TABLE OF CONTENTS

SPIDER-MAN 2™

THE GAME

OFFICIAL STRATEGY GUIDE

Introduction

THE STORY SO FAR...

When people bed down for the night in New York City, they do so with the comfort of knowing that Spider-Man is somewhere out there fighting to keep them safe. After all, it is the criminal mind that is the most nocturnal in this city that never sleeps. But how safe would these millions feel if they knew their famed superhero was distracted by girl trouble?

Peter Parker is now a college student busying himself with his studies and his two part-time jobs as a pizza delivery boy and photographer. And this says nothing of his crime-fighting duties. Mary Jane, the wondrous girl next door, is now starring in a play and has moved away from her troubled household. She has an apartment of her own in Soho. She's a smart and beautiful girl who is growing increasingly lonely with each passing night—she needs someone who won't mysteriously run off all the time.

Living two separate lives is taking its toll on Peter. Not only does he lack time for the people he loves, but his grades are also beginning to slip. This division eventually starts to tear at Peter's psyche, as a potential love interest and newfound nemesis pull him deeper into the lonely and secretive world of the superhero. The only thing pulling him back is his love of Mary Jane and his wish to lead a normal life as a college student.

Spider-Man 2 is not just a tale of a superhero's efforts to rid the world of diabolical super villains. It is also the story of a young man's efforts to find balance. Fate has brought tremendous powers and an accompanying sense of responsibility. And while destiny may have given birth to Spider-Man, it did not destroy Peter Parker. Your job is to see that it doesn't.

ABOUT THIS GUIDE

The book you now hold is your guide to living the ultimate life of a superhero in New York City. This book contains tips and strategies for every aspect of the game, from defeating each of the super villains to navigating the enormous city, to completing each and every one of the hundreds of side missions and Challenge races.

The book is divided into three main sections. The "Superhero Training" chapter contains everything you need to know about all of Spider-Man's amazing combat and movement techniques, in addition to the basic information about playing the game. The "Swing-Through" portion of the guide follows the main story arc and includes detailed, step-by-step strategies for completing every mission and requirement. The other main strategy-rich portion of the book is the chapter entitled "The Hero's Work is Never Done." There you will find dozens of pages of tips and maps that will help you earn that coveted Game Master award. Of course, there is also an Art Gallery, a two-sided poster, and a revealing look at all of the game's unlockable extras. Enjoy!

Cast of Characters

REPRESENTING GOOD...

SPIDER-MAN™

ON THE OUTSIDE, SPIDER-MAN IS AN EXTREMELY CONFIDENT, WITTY HERO POSSESSING TREMEN-DOUS STRENGTH AND AGILITY. HIS COURAGE SEEMS AS ENDLESS AS THE LIST OF CRIMINALS HE HAS THWARTED. BENEATH THE COSTUME, HOWEVER, LIES A MILD-MANNERED BOY BY THE NAME OF PETER PARKER. AS SPIDER-MAN, HE FEARLESSLY PLACES HIMSELF IN HARM'S WAY AND GOES TOE-TO-TOE WITH THE MEANEST SUPER VILLAINS EVER. AS PETER PARKER, HE LACKS THE NERVE TO ASK THE GIRL NEXT DOOR OUT ON A DATE. BALANCING THIS DICHOTOMY COULD PROVE TO BE SPIDER-MAN'S BIGGEST CHALLENGE YET.

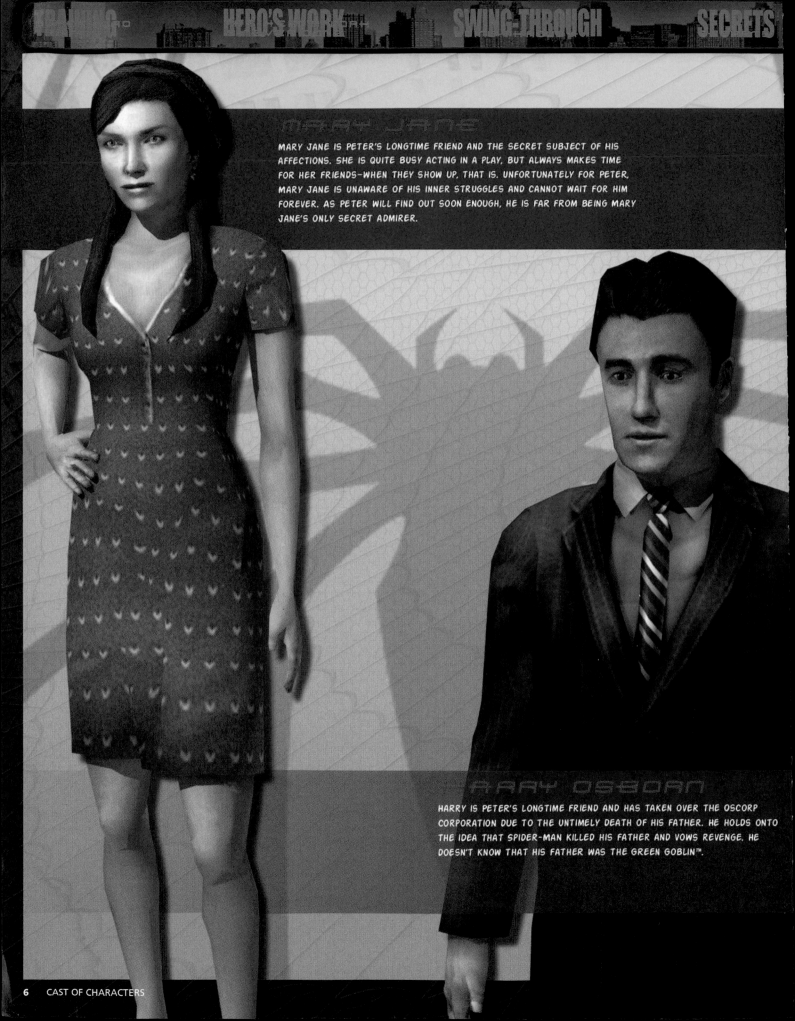

MARY JANE

MARY JANE IS PETER'S LONGTIME FRIEND AND THE SECRET SUBJECT OF HIS AFFECTIONS. SHE IS QUITE BUSY ACTING IN A PLAY, BUT ALWAYS MAKES TIME FOR HER FRIENDS—WHEN THEY SHOW UP, THAT IS. UNFORTUNATELY FOR PETER, MARY JANE IS UNAWARE OF HIS INNER STRUGGLES AND CANNOT WAIT FOR HIM FOREVER. AS PETER WILL FIND OUT SOON ENOUGH, HE IS FAR FROM BEING MARY JANE'S ONLY SECRET ADMIRER.

HARRY OSBORN

HARRY IS PETER'S LONGTIME FRIEND AND HAS TAKEN OVER THE OSCORP CORPORATION DUE TO THE UNTIMELY DEATH OF HIS FATHER. HE HOLDS ONTO THE IDEA THAT SPIDER-MAN KILLED HIS FATHER AND VOWS REVENGE. HE DOESN'T KNOW THAT HIS FATHER WAS THE GREEN GOBLIN™.

BLACK CAT™

BLACK CAT IS AN ENIGMA. RUMORS HAVE IT THAT HER REAL NAME IS FELICIA
HARDY BUT NOT MUCH ELSE IS KNOWN ABOUT THIS MYSTERIOUS CHARACTER.
BLACK CAT SHOWS UP IN THE DARK OF NIGHT AND OFTEN FLIRTATIOUSLY LEADS
SPIDER-MAN IN A ROMP ACROSS THE CITY. SHE CLAIMS TO NOT BE A CROOK
BUT, ODDLY ENOUGH, SHE ALWAYS KNOWS EXACTLY WHERE THE BAD GUYS ARE.
ALTHOUGH HER INTENTIONS ARE UNKNOWN, SPIDER-MAN COMES TO TRUST HER
DEEPLY AND WILL EVEN SEEK HER ADVICE.

REPRESENTING EVIL...

RHINO™

RHINO IS AN OVERSIZED, LUMBERING BRUTE WITH A PENCHANT FOR BODY ARMOR AND IVORY. HE'S UNDOUBTEDLY THE LEAST INTELLIGENT SUPER VILLAIN SPIDER-MAN HAS EVER FACED. RHINO PACKS QUITE A PUNCH AND HAS A SHARP, POINTY TUSK ON HIS HEAD, BUT HIS INABILITY TO KEEP FROM DIZZYING HIMSELF MAKES HIM A BIT OF A PUSHOVER.

QUENTIN BECH▶

THIS ARROGANT SPECIAL EFFECTS GURU HAS SUPPOSEDLY FLOWN OUT FROM HOLLYWOOD TO TRY AND PROVE THAT SPIDER-MAN IS A FRAUD. AS IF THAT WASN'T BAD ENOUGH, MR. JAMESON AT THE DAILY BUGLE ACTUALLY BELIEVES HIM!

MYSTERIO™

IN THE WORLD OF SUPER VILLAINS, FEW HAVE AS FITTING A NAME AS MYSTERIO. THIS CREATURE'S ORIGINS ARE UNKNOWN, AND EVERY ATTEMPT TO CAPTURE HIM IS FOILED BY HIS CONSTANT USE OF HOLOGRAMS. WHILE HIS IMAGE MAY NOT ALWAYS BE REAL, THE FLYING ROBOTS HE UNLEASHES ON NEW YORK CITY ARE BONA FIDE DELIVERERS OF LASER-FIRING TERROR, AND MUST BE STOPPED AT ALL COSTS.

DOC OCK™

THE MAN FORMERLY KNOWN AS DOCTOR OCTAVIUS SOUGHT TO MEET THE WORLD'S ENERGY NEEDS THROUGH SCIENCE. UNFORTUNATELY, A HORRIBLE ACCIDENT ALTERS HIS WAY OF LIFE, AND HE SOON SEEKS NOTHING BUT THE DEATH OF SPIDER-MAN. DOC OCK IS AN EXTREMELY STRONG, CUNNING ENEMY THAT RELIES ON THE FOUR TENTACLES HE WEARS TO PROVIDE HIM WITH SUPERHUMAN STRENGTH AND SPEED. HE IS SPIDER-MAN'S GREATEST THREAT YET.

SHOCKER™

SHOCKER IS A LONGTIME ENEMY OF SPIDER-MAN AND HAS FOUND HIS WAY OUT OF PRISON AND BACK ONTO THE STREETS. HE IS HIGHLY MOBILE AND HAS THE ABILITY TO LOB BALLS OF ENERGY DURING FIGHTS. AS IF THAT WASN'T BAD ENOUGH, HE CAN ALSO USE A SORT OF BEAM-LIKE ENERGY FIELD TO FORCE HIS ADVERSARY INTO THE AIR AS IF LEVITATING.

THE DAILY BUGLE

MR. JAMESON

JONAH JAMESON IS THE MOODY PUBLISHER IN CHARGE OF THE DAILY BUGLE. MR. JAMESON WILL NEVER ADMIT THAT HE LIKES PETER'S PHOTOS, BUT THAT DOESN'T STOP HIM FROM RUNNING THEM ON THE FRONT PAGE!

ROBBIE ROBERTSON

ROBBIE IS A BIG FAN OF PETER'S PHOTOGRAPHY AND WILL OFTEN BE READY TO GIVE PETER A PHOTO ASSIGNMENT SHOULD HE BE LOOKING FOR SOME EXTRA WORK.

BETTY BRANT

BETTY IS MR. JAMESON'S SECRETARY AND IS A VERY BUSY, BUT FRIENDLY LADY. SHE WOULDN'T MIND GOING OUT ON A DATE WITH PETER, AND SHE IS NOT SHY ABOUT HIM KNOWING IT.

THE SCIENTISTS

DR. CONNORS

DR. CONNORS IS PETER'S SCIENCE PROFESSOR AT THE UNIVERSITY. HE SEES THE POTENTIAL IN PETER, BUT CAN'T HELP WISHING THAT HE WOULD DO A BETTER JOB OF STAYING AWAKE IN HIS CLASS. DR. CONNORS IS A CLOSE FRIEND OF DR. OCTAVIUS.

DR. OCTAVIUS

DR. OCTAVIUS LIVES ON THE UPPER WEST SIDE IN A GLORIOUS APARTMENT THAT ALSO SERVES AS HIS RESEARCH LABORATORY. HE IS IN THE PROCESS OF CREATING A FUSION REACTOR THAT HE HOPES WILL SUPPLY ENDLESS ENERGY TO THE WORLD. HIS REACTOR RELIES ON A MATERIAL PROVIDED TO HIM BY HARRY OSBORN'S COMPANY.

ROSIE OCTAVIUS

ROSIE IS DR. OCTAVIUS'S WIFE, ASSISTANT, AND MUSE. SHE PROVIDES HIM WITH THE SUPPORT THAT KEEPS HIM HEALTHY DURING HIS LONG SESSIONS IN THE LAB.

Superhero Training

When Peter Parker was first bitten by the genetically engineered spider, and started to realize that he was capable of actions that no other human dared dream possible, the first thing he did was to go out in the city and test his new skills. He wasn't an instant master at Wall Crawling and Web Swinging, but he practiced and soon became very comfortable with his new abilities. And so you must practice.

Spider-Man has tremendous powers, many of which are available at the start of the game, and although the controls are responsive and intuitive, moving him through the city with style and speed only comes with time. This chapter contains all there is to know about putting Spider-Man's movement abilities to use in the streets and on the rooftops of New York City.

Of course, Spider-Man isn't swinging around the city merely for the fun of it—although it is very enjoyable. He may consider the city his playground, but he has taken on the responsibility of helping the citizens who live here when nobody else can. This often requires him to mix it up with criminals and thugs who feel the law doesn't apply to them. As you can imagine, Spider-Man has an amazing assortment of attacks and combos that he can use to thwart the city's crooks, each of which are explained in full detail in the following pages.

Locomotion Abilities

Spider-Man has several abilities that elevate him to superhero status. While his Web Swinging talents are universally known, he has many other skills including Wallsprinting, Wall Crawling, Poleswinging, and several others. The following controls can be used at any time to help move Spider-Man around the city. All of these techniques are available to Spider-Man at the start of the game.

RUNNING

Running on the street is the slowest way to cover long distances, but it is still necessary from time to time. Use the Movement Controls to direct Spider-Man in your chosen direction and to make him run or walk. Hold the Sprint Button to make him sprint.

JUMPING

Spider-Man can leap with the best of them! Tap the Jump Button to make him hop in place, or keep the Jump Button depressed to charge the Jump Meter. Release the Jump Button to send him flying several stories into the air. It's possible to use a fully charged jump while sprinting to cover huge distances in a single bound. Similarly, Spider-Man can leap while Wall Crawling, Wall Sliding, Wallsprinting, Poleswinging, and Web Swinging. Press the Jump Button just as Spider-Man lands to make him perform a Double Jump; this is great while sprinting when there are no tall buildings to which he can attach a Web Line.

WALL CRAWLING

One of Spider-Man's most famous abilities is his capacity to attach onto a wall and crawl along any surface regardless if it's horizontal, vertical, or inverted. To do so, simply approach the wall and press the Grab Button. This makes Spider-Man grab onto the surface with both hands and feet. Use the Movement Controls to climb. Hold the Sprint Button to make him crawl faster, or use the Jump Button to make him leap along the face of the surface—this is a very quick way to Wall Crawl up a skyscraper.

WALLSPRINTING

Arguably one of the slickest moves in Spider-Man's repertoire is the ability to sprint along the side of a building. Jump or Web Swing toward a building, hold the Sprint Button as Spider-Man approaches, and then press the Grab Button as Spider-Man touches the building to make him Wallsprint. He'll eventually run out of steam and start to slip, so be prepared to jump or transition to a Wall Crawl. Spider-Man can Wallsprint in any direction, including down toward the street.

GOING VERTICAL

Try Wallsprinting up the side of a building while charging the Jump Meter, and then leap straight up into another Wallsprint. There's no faster way to scale a skyscraper!

WALL SLIDING

When it's time to descend off a building, look no further than the Wall Slide. Sure, Spider-Man can always dive off a rooftop and hope to Web Swing to safety, but the Wall Slide is a way to descend at a safe, controlled rate (perfect for Pizza Delivery Missions). To perform the Wall Slide, simply press the Movement Controls toward an adjacent building face and watch as Spider-Man uses the sides of his feet to slow his descent.

WALL JUMPING

Press the Jump Button during a Wall Slide to make Spider-Man propel himself off the building's side and into the air. Use the Wall Slide to descend to the desired height, and then Wall Jump into a Web Swing to continue traveling to the destination. This is a great way to maintain momentum.

WEB SWINGING

Spider-Man's signature move is the Web Swing. Leap into the air and press the Swing Button to make Spider-Man shoot a Web Line at a nearby building (or any other tall object, including trees and flagpoles). Watch in awe as he swings high above the ground like a pendulum. Use the Movement Controls to add momentum to Spider-Man's swinging, and press the Jump Button to exit the swing. Each time the Swing Button is pressed, Spider-Man will shoot another Web Line. Angle Spider-Man around a corner or across the street while pressing the Swing Button to direct him through the maze of Manhattan streets. Timing is critical, though. Practice releasing from a Web Line at different points in the swing arc to see where momentum sends Spider-Man. Similarly, rounding corners takes some practice to get a feel for when to shoot the next Web Line.

MAXIMUM MOMENTUM

When used in conjunction with the Sprint Button and Jump Button, Web Swinging can be used to cover tremendous ground in a short amount of time. For starters, as soon as Spider-Man begins to Web Swing, charge the Jump Meter to prepare for the dismount. While holding the Jump Button, hold the Sprint Button to gain a Swing Boost. Now, while pressing forward on the Movement Controls, release the Jump Button just as Spider-Man begins to swing upward (about the 7 o'clock position). This sends him flying through the air with all the momentum gained from the Web Swing. Fire the next Web Line just as gravity begins to take hold, and begin holding the Jump and Sprint buttons again.

POLESWINGING

See all those flagpoles and lampposts everywhere? Well, Spider-Man can swing from those like an Olympic gymnast! Leap toward any horizontal pole and press the Grab Button to make Spider-Man grab hold and start Poleswinging. Press Up on the Movement Controls to keep Spider-Man's momentum going. Or pull Down to make him come to a stop and perch atop the pole. Release the Grab Button while Poleswinging to send Spider-Man flying into the air. Poleswinging is a great way to gain a lot of momentum when first transitioning from the street into a Web Swing.

LOCOMOTION UPGRADES

Beginning in Chapter 2, Spider-Man can visit various Upgrade Stores throughout the city to spend his hard-earned Hero Points on Hero Upgrades. Many of these upgrades concern his combat skills, but plenty add speed and style to his travels across the city.

SWING SPEED UPGRADES

Each successive upgrade increases Spider-Man's swing speed. The costlier upgrades prove indispensable in completing many of the later Photo Missions, Challenges, and Pizza Missions. Don't even think about trying the "Insane" Challenges without the highest Swing Speed upgrades.

SWING SPEED LEVEL	COST (HERO POINTS)	AVAILABILITY
1	50	Chapter 2
2	1000	Chapter 3
3	1250	Chapter 6
4	1500	Chapter 7
5	2000	Chapter 9
6	5000	Chapter 13
7	20,000	Chapter 16
8	50,000	Chapter 17

WALLSPRINT DURATION UPGRADE

LEVEL	COST (HERO POINTS)	AVAILABILITY
1	1000	Chapter 7
2	15,000	*

This upgrade increases the amount of time that Spider-Man can Wallsprint before gravity takes hold. This upgrade is vital for maximizing Spider-Man's speed and maneuverability.

WEB ZIP

Cost: 1000 Hero Points
Availability: Chapter 3

Press the Web Swing Button while holding the Sprint Button to Web Zip. This is arguably the most important Hero Upgrade to acquire early in the game, as it allows Spider-Man to move rapidly in a horizontal direction across almost any terrain. Spider-Man shoots a Web Line directly ahead and then yanks on it to catapult himself forward in a straight line. It's perfect for reaching faraway rooftops or to cross Central Park through the treetops without Web Swinging.

SLINGSHOT JUMP

Cost: 600 Hero Points
Availability: Chapter 3

While holding two webs, swing back and Charge Jump to get extra jump distance.

AIR TRICK: INVERTED WIDOW

Cost: 250 Hero Points
Availability: Chapter 4

Press the Jump Button in the middle of Double Jumping to perform this acrobatic trick.

AIR TRICK: SUPER FLY SPIDER GUY

Cost: 250 Hero Points
Availability: Chapter 4

Press the Jump Button in the middle of a Falling Twirl to perform this acrobatic trick.

AIR TRICK: WEB FREAK TANGO

Cost: 250
Availability: Chapter 8

Press Jump (x2) in the middle of a Falling Twirl to perform this acrobatic trick (must first purchase Super Fly Spider Guy).

AIR TRICK: DADDY LONG LEGS

Cost: 250
Availability: Chapter 8

Press Jump (x2) in the middle of Double Jumping to perform this acrobatic trick (must first purchase Inverted Widow).

AIR TRICK: MANHATTAN WEB ROLL

Cost: 500
Availability: Chapter 10

Press Jump (x3) in the middle of a Falling Twirl to perform this acrobatic trick (must first purchase Web Freak Tango).

AIR TRICK: THE SPINNARET

Cost: 500
Availability: Chapter 10

Press Jump (x3) in the middle of Double Jumping to perform this acrobatic trick (must first purchase Daddy Long Legs).

AIR TRICK: THE ROLLING REPORTER

Cost: 1000
Availability: Chapter 12

Press Jump (x4) in the middle of Double Jumping to perform this acrobatic trick (must first purchase The Spinnaret).

AIR TRICK: WEBTASTIC 360

Cost: 1500
Availability: Chapter 14

Press Jump (x5) in the middle of Double Jumping to perform this acrobatic trick (must first purchase The Rolling Reporter).

AIR TRICK: THE POISON PIKE

Cost: 2000
Availability: Chapter 15

Press Jump (x6) in the middle of Double Jumping to perform this acrobatic trick (must first purchase Webtastic 360).

Spider-Man™ in Combat

Spider-Man is an accomplished brawler. He relies on a wealth of combat abilities when he mixes it up with the city's ruffians. He has specific attacks that he can perform on the ground, in the air, and still others that can be done only when he's using his Spider Reflexes or when counterattacking. The following attacks and dodges are separated based on their applicable situation. All of the following attacks are available at the start of the game.

SPIDER REFLEXES

Spider-Man has the uncanny ability to slow down the apparent movement of those around him while simultaneously heightening his own awareness and speeding his actions. This allows him to sense and dodge incoming attacks before they occur. Spider Reflexes also buys him the necessary time to unleash devastating combos on his opponents. Press the Spider Reflexes Button to trigger this unique ability, but beware that Spider-Man can remain in this state for only so long. Monitor the blue meter in the HUD to gauge how much longer he can use his Spider Reflexes. When not in use, this meter fills up over time, based on the amount of style that Spider-Man incorporates into his travels.

TRY LAUNCHING YOURSELF FROM A WEB BY CHARGE JUMPING WHILE SWINGING!

ATTACK EFFECTS

Many of Spider-Man's attacks have a specific result, known as an effect. There are six primary effects that an attack can have:

1. **Escape:** Creates distance by moving Spider-Man away.
2. **Air Combat:** Leads naturally into air combat.
3. **Clearing:** Hits multiple enemies to clear room for Spider-Man.
4. **Distance:** Creates distance for Spider-Man by moving enemy far away.
5. **Disable:** Temporarily disables enemy so Spider-Man can deal with others.
6. **Range:** Can initiate an attack from a distance.

Basic Attacks when Standing, Running, or Wall Crawling

ATTACK NAME	CONTROLS	EFFECT
Targeting System	Down	N/A
Right Hook	Attack	N/A
Left Hook	Attack, Attack	N/A
Hop-Over Head Punch	Attack, Jump	Escape
Web Trip	Attack, Web	N/A
Knockdown Punch	Attack, Attack, Attack	N/A
Jump-Off Kick	Attack, Attack, Jump	Escape
Web Hammer	Attack, Attack, Web	N/A
Link to Web Rodeo	Attack, Attack, Web (while rotating Movement Controls)	Clearing, Distance
Web Blind/Disarm/Trap	Web (tap to blind/disarm, hold to trap)	N/A, Disable
Yank Up	Web + Up	Air Combat
Yank Toward Self	Web + Down	Air Combat, Range
Yank Left	Web + Left	Distance
Yank Right	Web + Right	Distance
Web Rodeo	Web + rotate Movement Controls	Clearing, Distance
Yank Kick	Web, Attack	N/A
Thrust Kick	Web, Attack, Attack	N/A
Web Blast	Web, Attack, Web	Distance

Spider Reflexes Attacks when Standing, Running, or Wall Crawling

ATTACK NAME	CONTROLS	EFFECT
Punch	Attack	N/A
Drop Kick	Attack, Attack	N/A
Mule Kick	Attack, Attack, Attack	N/A

Basic Airborne Attacks

ATTACK NAME	CONTROLS	EFFECT
Air Punch 1	Jump, Attack	N/A
Air Punch 2	Jump, Attack, Attack	N/A

Airborne Spider Reflexes Attacks

ATTACK NAME	CONTROLS	EFFECT
Air Kick	Jump, Attack	N/A
Air Flip Kick	Jump, Attack, Attack	N/A

Basic Attack when Sprinting

ATTACK NAME	CONTROLS	EFFECT
Rising Uppercut	Attack (hold to rise with enemy)	Air Combat, Escape

SPIDER REFLEXES

Spider Reflexes Attack when Sprinting

ATTACK NAME	CONTROLS	EFFECT
Rising Uppercut	Attack (hold to rise with enemy)	Air Combat, Escape

DODGING AND COUNTERATTACKS

Dodging and Counterattacks

ATTACK NAME	CONTROLS	EFFECT
Dodge Back	Grab (when red halo appears)	N/A
Dodge Back	Grab + Up (when red halo appears)	N/A
Dodge Back	Grab + Down (when red halo appears)	N/A
Dodge Left	Grab + Left (when red halo appears)	N/A
Dodge Right	Grab + Right (when red halo appears)	N/A
Counter Flip Kick	Grab, Attack (after successful Dodge Back)	N/A
Counter Flip Kick	Grab + Up, Attack (after successful Dodge Back)	N/A
Counter Flip Kick	Grab + Down, Attack (after successful Dodge Back)	N/A
Counter Elbow	Grab + Left, Attack (after successful Dodge Left)	N/A
Counter Uppercut	Grab + Right, Attack (after successful Dodge Right)	N/A

COMBAT UPGRADES

Beginning in Chapter 2, Spider-Man can visit various Upgrade Stores located throughout the city to purchase Hero Upgrades. The majority of these upgrades add new combo attacks and battle abilities to Spider-Man's crime-fighting repertoire. Visit an Upgrade Store at least once during every other chapter to stay current with all the available Hero Upgrades.

GRAPPLE

Cost: 750 Hero Points
Availability: Chapter 3

	CONTROLS	STATE	EFFECT
	Web, Grab	Standing/ Running/Crawling	Range

Hold the Web and Grab Buttons to reel enemies into your grasp.

AIR JUMP-OFF KICK

Cost: 1000 Hero Points
Availability: Chapter 4

	CONTROLS	STATE	EFFECT
	Jump (during a combo attack)	Air	Escape

At any point in an air combo, press the Jump Button to execute a kick that propels you higher into the air.

CANNONBALL KICK

Cost: 500 Hero Points
Availability: Chapter 4

	CONTROLS	STATE	EFFECT
	Attack	Swinging	N/A

Press the Attack Button while swinging to execute a swinging kick that hits multiple enemies.

MULTI-WEB TIE UPGRADES

MULTI-WEB TIE LEVEL	COST (HERO POINTS)	AVAILABILITY
1	1500	Chapter 4
2	2000	Chapter 7
3	2000	Chapter 9

Each successive upgrade increases the number of Web Lines Spider-Man can shoot to tie up enemies. When starting out, Spider-Man can Web Tie only a single enemy. But over time, he can acquire upgrades that allow him to Web Tie up to four enemies at once. Press the Web Button to begin tying up one enemy. Then press and hold the Web Button again to Web Tie additional enemies.

AIR COMBO UPGRADES

AIR COMBO LEVEL	COST (HERO POINTS)	AVAILABILITY
3	1000	Chapter 5
4	2000	Chapter 8

Spider-Man begins the game with the ability to leap into the air and strike an enemy with a vicious two-punch combo. Purchasing these upgrades allows Spider-Man to extend his Air Combo to include three and then ultimately four hits.

RISING KNEE KICK

Cost: 1000 Hero Points
Availability: Chapter 5

CONTROLS	STATE	EFFECT
Attack, Web, Jump	Standing/Running /Crawling	Escape, Air Combat

Press Attack, Web, Jump to knock your target into the air with a powerful knee attack.

YANK BEHIND

Cost: 500 Hero Points
Availability: Chapter 5

CONTROLS	STATE	EFFECT
Attack, Web, Grab	Standing/Running /Crawling	Distance, Clearing

Press Attack, Web, Grab to Web Yank your target and hit enemies behind you.

EARTH BREAKER PUNCH

Cost: 1250 Hero Points
Availability: Chapter 5

CONTROLS	STATE	EFFECT
Web, Attack, Jump	Standing/Running /Crawling	Clearing

Press Web, Attack, Jump to strike the ground with great force.

LAUNCH KICK

Cost: 750 Hero Points
Availability: Chapter 5

CONTROLS	STATE	EFFECT
Attack, Jump	Dodge/ Counterattacking	Air Combat

After dodging an attack, press Attack, Jump to knock your target into the air.

DIZZY STRIKE

Cost: 1000
Availability: Chapter 6

CONTROLS	STATE	EFFECT
Attack, Attack, Grab	Standing/Running /Crawling	Disable

Press Attack, Attack, Grab to stun the target and leave him dizzy for some time.

THE HERO PUNCH

Cost: 1250
Availability: Chapter 7

CONTROLS	STATE	EFFECT
Attack	Full Jump Meter	Clearing

Fully charge the Jump Meter and then press the Attack Button to knock the enemies away.

INTERCEPTOR KICK

Cost: 1000
Availability: Chapter 8

CONTROLS	STATE	EFFECT
Web, Attack, Web, Attack	Standing/Running /Crawling	Clearing, Escape

Press Web, Attack, Web, Attack to perform this long-range attack with great power.

MULTI-WEB HAMMER

Cost: 1500
Availability: Chapter 9

CONTROLS	STATE	EFFECT
Attack, Attack, Web	Standing/Running /Crawling	N/A

Press Attack, Attack, Web (can press Web up to 6x) to smash the target into the ground multiple times.

JAW LAUNCHER

Cost: 1000
Availability: Chapter 9

CONTROLS	STATE	EFFECT
Attack, Attack, Jump	Spider Reflexes	Air Combat, Escape

Press Attack, Attack, Jump during Spider Reflexes to launch enemy into the air.

AIR PILE DRIVER

Cost: 1250
Availability: Chapter 9

CONTROLS	STATE	EFFECT
Grab	Air Grapple	N/A

Press the Grab Button while grappling an enemy in the air to execute a spinning pile driver (must first purchase the Grapple). Can tap the Grab Button repeatedly to inflict greater damage.

DOUBLE HEEL KICK

Cost: 1000
Availability: Chapter 10

CONTROLS	STATE	EFFECT
Attack, Attack, Grab, Attack	Standing/Running /Crawling	N/A

Press Attack, Attack, Grab, Attack to execute a hacking heel kick (must first purchase Dizzy Strike).

STAIR STEP KICKS COMBO

Cost: 1250
Availability: Chapter 10

CONTROLS	STATE	EFFECT
Attack, Attack, Jump, Attack	Spider Reflexes	N/A

Press Attack, Attack, Jump, and then Attack rapidly during Spider Reflexes to execute many kicks on the enemy (must first purchase Jaw Launcher).

WHIRLWIND KICK

Cost: 3000
Availability: Chapter 10

CONTROLS	STATE	EFFECT
Attack, Attack	Dodge/ Counterattacking	Clearing

Press Attack, Attack after dodging an attack to execute a very powerful clearing kick.

AIR WEB SLAM

Cost: 1500
Availability: Chapter 10

CONTROLS	STATE	EFFECT
Web	Air Grapple	Distance

Press the Web Button while grappling an enemy in the air to spin flip the enemy using a Web Line (must first purchase Grapple).

WEB HANGER

Cost: 2500
Availability: Chapter 11

CONTROLS	STATE	EFFECT
Attack, Attack, Web, Jump	Grapple	Escape, Disable

Press Attack, Attack, Web, Jump to web unconscious enemies up to light posts and traffic lights.

SUPER WEB

Cost: 1500
Availability: Chapter 11

CONTROLS	STATE	EFFECT
Web, Attack, Web, Web	Standing/Running /Crawling	Disable

Press Web, Attack, Web, Web to disable enemies by engulfing them in a Super Web attack.

RISING SHOULDER CHARGE

Cost: 2500
Availability: Chapter 13

CONTROLS	STATE	EFFECT
Attack	Sprinting with Full Jump Meter	N/A

Fully charge a Jump, then press the Attack Button while sprinting to knock enemies away and get up into the air.

SPIDER MISSILE

Cost: 1500
Availability: Chapter 13

CONTROLS	STATE	EFFECT
Attack	Wallsprinting/ Wall Jumping	N/A

Press the Attack Button while Wallsprinting or Wall Jumping to execute a fast homing attack.

Hero Points, Tokens, Icons, and More

HERO POINTS

Hero Points are Spider-Man's currency. He can spend them at any of the dozens of Upgrade Stores throughout the city to purchase Hero Upgrades and to acquire a Full Health recovery. Hero Points are earned by completing tasks as simple as triggering Hint Markers to deeds as dangerous as defeating the city's most diabolical scum. In short, Spider-Man earns Hero Points for almost everything he does. Look for the yellow numbers to appear on the screen after defeating enemies or completing objectives. The upper number is Spider-Man's current total, and the lower number shows the amount of Hero Points he just earned.

Nearly every chapter in the game has a Hero Point requirement listed in the To-Do List (accessible via the Pause Menu). This ensures that the player always has enough Hero Points to purchase the newest and best Hero Upgrades that become available in the next chapter. See the "Spider-Man's Free Time" section at the conclusion of each chapter in the walkthrough for tips on earning the specified number of Hero Points.

TOKENS AND ICONS

Spider-Man encounters a number of brightly lit tokens and icons throughout the city during his adventures. While collecting many of these tokens is purely optional (e.g. Secret Tokens, Skyscraper Tokens, Buoy Tokens, etc.) nearly every type of token nets Spider-Man several Hero Points as a reward for finding it. Other icons are even more beneficial to his well being.

HEALTH ICON
Spider-Man won't find these bright red icons lying in plain sight on the city streets and rooftops; they appear only after he has completed a Voluntary

Mission, Petty Crime, or primary mission with a battle in it. Wait around for a moment to watch for a Health Icon to drop out of the sky, and then grab it to refill Spider-Man's Health Meter.

A WORD ABOUT DEATH

Mortality is a serious matter, but because this is a videogame it needn't be permanent. If Spider-Man's Health Meter runs empty, you'll have to continue the game—usually from a part of the city some distance from where Spider-Man met his demise. Should Spider-Man falter during a mission, the player will be faced with an option to retry the mission or to start the chapter anew, but Spider-Man will lose 100 Hero Points as a penalty.

FULL HEALTH RECOVERY

If you're running low on health and worried about falling in an upcoming battle, or literally falling from a skyscraper, head to a nearby Upgrade Store and purchase a Full Health Recovery. It costs one Hero Point per point of health recovered, but it's a small price to pay for eternal longevity.

CHANGE ICON
One can't run around in red and blue tights forever; occasionally Peter Parker has to ditch his costume and resume the life of a normal college student. Numerous missions involve swinging to a specific destination where a Change Icon is located. Approach the icon and press the Attack Button to change back to Peter Parker. Although this usually leads directly into a cutscene, you will have control of Peter Parker inside the Daily Bugle.

HINT MARKERS
There are 213 Hint Markers located throughout the city, each of which awards Spider-Man 10 Hero Points in addition to providing some valuable advice. These green markers are found sitting in plain view on the street corners, in alleys, and on

rooftops. Access the Zoom Map and toggle over to the Hint Marker screen to see the distribution of Hint Markers across the map. Those that Spider-Man has already visited will be outlined in yellow.

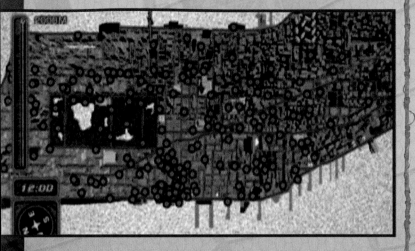

DESTINATION MARKERS

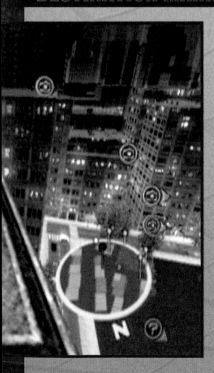

New York City is a huge place. It's several times larger than nearly every other city in the United States, with Chicago and Los Angeles being notable exceptions. As you can probably imagine, getting Spider-Man from one end of the city to a specific rooftop miles away could be quite difficult. Thankfully, the game has a very helpful system of Destination Markers. They appear both on the screen as a part of the HUD and in the Zoom Map and Mini Map. They indicate the direction that Spider-Man must travel to reach his next objective. The Mini Map also provides lines that illustrate the Destination Marker's elevation.

Destination Markers appear in a variety of colors, with each representing a different level of urgency or importance.

BLUE DESTINATION MARKERS

These represent the highest priority destinations and are often accompanied by a timer. Blue Destination Markers correspond to key missions and cannot be ignored. In fact, Spider-Man cannot access any Challenges or other side missions when a blue Destination Marker is on the screen.

YELLOW DESTINATION MARKERS

Yellow Destination Markers often correspond to a side mission objective. They are used to point out the location of an enemy or marker during a secondary mission, such as during a Challenge or a Voluntary Mission. Yellow Destination Markers guide Spider-Man to where the action is.

WHITE DESTINATION MARKERS

These Destination Markers correspond to goals that Spider-Man must meet to complete the To-Do List Requirements. They are never urgent, but Spider-Man must reach the location eventually if he's to complete the chapter. Consider exploring the city and completing Voluntary Missions or Challenges whenever a white Destination Marker is on the screen, as it means that Spider-Man has some free time.

Training Games at the Arcade

The arcade has several games specifically designed to help Spider-Man train for combat. Each arcade game reinforces a different area of combat. Consider swinging by the arcade in the early stages to check out the games. Although only one game is available at the start, completing each game unlocks the next one. Completing all four arcade games earns Spider-Man the "Hardcore Gamer" award.

DODGE HALL

Spider-Man is placed in a narrow corridor opposite an armed enemy. Watch for Spider-Man's head to flash from his Spider Senses, and quickly press the Grab Button to dodge the incoming bullet. There are two rounds of competition, but it all boils

down to pressing the Grab Button fast enough to dodge the bullets. Spider-Man can get hit twice and still win the game but don't get hit a third time, or it will be game over!

DIRECTIONAL ATTACK

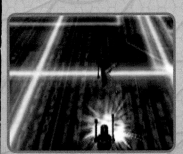

This game takes place in a large arena. Spider-Man stands face-to-face with an enemy, and a second one approaches from behind as Spider-Man hits the one he faces. Quickly attack the one in front by pressing the Attack Button, then immediately press Down on the Movement Controls, and press the Attack Button again to quickly attack the enemy behind Spider-Man. Directional Attacks work only if they come during a combo, so make sure you press those buttons quickly.

WEB ATTACK

This game provides an overview of the basic web attacks. There are three rounds to complete: the first deals with the Web Tie attack, the second with the Web Yank, and the third with using the Web Button to disarm enemies. Robots advance toward Spider-Man one at a time from different directions. Turn in place, and press and hold the Web Button to Web Tie them before they reach Spider-Man. To Web Yank enemies, hold the Web Button to Web Tie them, and then press the Movement Controls in the direction you wish to pull them. To disarm an enemy of his weapon, simply face him and tap the Web Button.

AIR COMBO

This game teaches Spider-Man how to launch enemies into the air and then beat the daylights out of them while they're airborne. There are three basic ways to get an enemy into the air. The first way is to Sprint toward the enemy and press the Attack Button to perform the Sprint Uppercut. Another way is to begin to Web Tie the enemy, and then press Up on the Movement Controls to Web Yank him into the air. Finally, Spider-Man can leap into the air and then Web Yank an enemy up to him by pressing Down on the Movement Controls while performing the Web Tie. Once an enemy is in the air, all Spider-Man has to do is get close to him and pummel him with a series of punches and kicks. Just keep pressing the Attack Button until the thug is incapacitated.

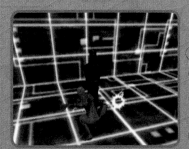

Battle Tips

Spider-Man is very strong and agile, so he typically has little trouble defeating the lowlife thugs that threaten the city's peace. His numerous combo attacks, ability to Web Trap enemies, and his time-altering Spider Reflexes make it unlikely that any mere mortal can defeat him in a one-on-one fight. The perps of the city know this and will gradually begin to attack in greater and greater numbers. No matter how many Hero Upgrades Spider-Man purchases, taking on a half dozen or more criminals—some of them with guns—isn't a walk in the park. Keep the following tips in mind when stepping into tougher battles.

FOREVER DODGING
It's important to rapidly tap the Grab Button when confronted by a number of enemies with guns. The bullets whiz by at a fast rate, and the only way to time button presses with Spider-Man's ever-flashing head is to repeatedly tap the button. This fills the blue Spider Reflexes meter faster, too.

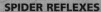

KEEP MOVING!
Staying on the move is important, as it keeps Spider-Man from being surrounded. Continually run and jump, and try to use the Web Yank attack to pull enemies to Spider-Man. Don't forget to use the powerful clearing attacks, such as the Hero Punch and Rising Shoulder Charge to send multiple enemies flying.

SPIDER REFLEXES
Spider Reflexes should be used whenever Spider-Man is in a tough battle. It makes dodging bullets and other attacks simpler, and Spider-Man's attacks inflict more damage during Spider Reflexes.

AIR COMBO POWER
Always remember that Air Combos inflict more damage than ground-based combos. Air Combos make it easier to finish off enemies, and Spider-Man is also safer when airborne. Although he's still be vulnerable to gunfire, most enemies don't carry guns.

The Hero's Work is Never Done

Spider-Man 2: The Game offers a lot more gameplay than the missions that develop the gripping storyline. In fact, the actual story chapters of the game make up less than half of the total gameplay. Wondering where that other half of the game comes from? Well, look no further than this chapter because it's all here. There are enough challenges to complete and items to collect to keep someone busy for quite some time. Throw in the city's never-ending supply of criminal activity and it should be obvious why this chapter is titled 'The Hero's Work is Never Done.' That's because it never is, especially with that whole "great power, great responsibility" bit.

Voluntary Missions

As a superhero, Spider-Man has a duty not only to uphold the law, but also to make sure that others do so. Sure, the city has its own police force, but if there's one thing Spider-Man learned since discovering his powers, it's that the police can't be expected to be everywhere at once. Spider-Man can volunteer to fill in for the police whenever they are busy.

CITIZENS IN DISTRESS

How Spider-Man goes about helping the citizens of New York City depends on how he learns of their trouble. Those people with the green question marks above their heads are considered "Citizens in Distress." Although they will call out to Spider-Man for help, they will not tell him what to do until he stops to talk to them. Citizens in Distress appear at random throughout the city and are the primary type of crime-fighting voluntary mission.

The people of New York City find themselves in all sorts of crises, so there is certainly no shortage of variety. Spider-Man encounters one of any number of situations whenever he stops to help a Citizen in Distress. He can expect to meet the following situations, all of which help increase his Hero Point tally.

ROBBERY
Robberies often involve multiple thugs and an armored car. Spider-Man must defeat the thugs and retrieve the stolen bag of money. Sometimes the thugs flee the scene in a getaway car, and other times they may even escape in an helicopter. Either way, the mission doesn't end until Spider-Man retrieves the money. Spider-Man can earn some extra Hero Points by untying the drivers of the armored car before leaving.

MEDICAL EMERGENCY
In this situation, Spider-Man has to pick up a pedestrian and race to the hospital before time runs out. Press Web + ↑ to pick up the injured person, and then Web Swing as fast as possible toward the Destination Marker. Although Spider-Man does not suffer damage from extreme falls when he's carrying a patient, he cannot use his Web Zip ability.

OFFICER ASSIST MISSIONS
Show the people of New York City that Spider-Man is invaluable by rescuing police stuck behind their car, avoiding gunfire from nearby thugs. Rush to the scene to disarm and incapacitate the thugs to help out the cops.

CARJACKING MISSIONS
The cops are hot on the tail of a fleeing carjacker but Spider-Man can bring the chase to an end even faster. Run and leap onto the fleeing car and repeatedly press the Attack Button to disable it and make it stop. Watch for Spider-Man's trademark head flash, and quickly press the Grab Button to dodge a stray bullet from the driver's compartment.

AMBUSH
Sometimes gangs of thugs make an innocent pedestrian call for Spider-Man. The gang then leaps out of hiding and tries to bring down Spider-Man. Never approach a Citizen in Distress without a decent supply of health for this very reason.

SINKING SHIP

There is a ship starting to sink and Spider-Man is the only one who can save the passengers. Run and jump onto the ship, grab the passengers one at a time, and leap back to solid ground with them. Continue this until the entire crew is saved.

EXECUTE A CHARGED DOUBLE JUMP WHILE SPRINTING TO REACH THE BOAT

ALIENS AND/OR ARMORED BATTLE SUITS ATTACK

You'll encounter all walks of life in New York City, and although you may have never expected to encounter flying alien robots or giant Armored Battle Suits, it is a distinct possibility. Beat them into submission before it's too late.

DANGLING PEOPLE

It's not terribly common, but every now and then Spider-Man encounters someone dangling from a rooftop. Quickly Wallsprint or Web Swing up to the hapless sap, and press the Web Button to get hold of him. Wall Slide down the building's side to lower him safely to the ground.

PETTY CRIMES

Not every type of crime occurs with a warning. Sometimes, Spider-Man will be swinging along, minding his own business, when he'll hear a cry for help from a crime already in progress. If he's close to the crime scene, Spider-Man can track these "Petty Crimes" via the purple Destination Marker that appears onscreen. Petty Crimes are typically not as difficult as the missions given out by the Citizens in Distress, but they also reward fewer Hero Points. The following types of Petty Crimes are the most prevalent.

PURSE-SNATCHER

Purse-snatchers are overrunning the city. Listen for cries for help from a lone woman, and swing to her aid. Rush the thug and defeat him to gain the purse, and then return it to the woman.

LOST BALLOON

Little boys and girls sometimes lose their balloons. As a true hero, Spider-Man will stop what he's doing and get their balloon back for them. Get to a nearby rooftop, locate the balloon, and then make a jump for it. Spider-Man should try to leap directly at it, as all but the shortest of Web Lines will pop the balloon and make the child *really* cry.

ROAD RAGE

A driver suffering from road rage is yelling at everyone and driving unsafely. Stop him by leaping onto his car and punching it until the car stops. The driver won't be happy about the damage to his car, but at least he won't hurt anyone.

MUGGING

Sometimes the thugs get a little bolder, and rather than try to steal a purse from a lone woman, they'll gang up on a lone man and try to steal his wallet. Rush to his rescue and defeat the thugs (usually just three thugs).

GANG WARS

Spider-Man occasionally happens upon two rival gangs about to square off and fight one another. Both gangs turn their attention on Spider-Man when he arrives, so either flee to a safer area, or get ready for a brawl with a large number of armed thugs.

MISSION SUCCESS : EVERYONES HAPPY

BREAK-IN

Notice a bunch of thugs where they don't belong? Well, they're not supposed to be there. Get on the roof and take out each of them before they rob the store.

Pizza Missions

Peter Parker is always trying to balance his studies with his life as Spider-Man, but he also must earn money to pay the rent. Fortunately for him, starting in Chapter 3, he can visit Mr. Aziz at the pizza parlor

any time he wants and deliver some pizzas for him. Mr. Aziz has specific customer locations picked out ahead of time, and he also has a set time limit for each delivery run. Spider-Man must return to the pizza parlor after delivering all of the pizzas before the time runs out to complete the mission.

Each successful Pizza Mission not only nets Spider-Man a Hero Points bonus, but each happy customer also tips Spider-Man 10 Hero Points. Not every customer is happy, however. Spider-Man must avoid flipping and somersaulting when delivering the pizzas. He can "jostle" the pizzas only a total of three times during the delivery run. A fourth jostle sufficiently mangles the pizzas, and Mr. Aziz receives complaints. The mission is completed successfully only if Spider-Man delivers all pizzas in time, all the customers are happy, and he returns the empty bag in time.

The following table provides an outline of the data pertinent to each Pizza Mission. Note that the Pizza Missions increase in difficulty very swiftly and that even the fourth mission may prove too difficult without the Level 5 Swing Speed Upgrade.

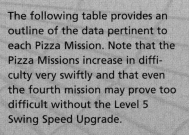

Pizza Mission Data

MISSION #	# OF PIZZAS	DELIVERY DISTANCES	TIME LIMIT	NOTES	HERO POINTS EARNED
1	1	268.0	2:00	A nearby delivery with plenty of time.	250
2	2	558.2, 572.6	1:50	Head north along the water for the first delivery, and then loop around to the right to drop off the second pizza.	300
3	2	204.4, 346.2	1:20	Web Swing and leap over the buildings due east of the pizza parlor to make both deliveries.	350
4	2	276.4, 324.0	1:25	Make the further delivery first, and then loop around to the alley to make the second delivery.	400
5	2	821.2, 1042.0	2:20	Web Swing north along the river to the nearer of the two locations. Then head east toward Central Park.	450
6	3	287.6, 435.5, 649.9	1:40	This is the first mission with three deliveries. Head to the nearby Comic Shop first and then head north.	500
7	3	491.8, 692.8, 714.5	1:45	Deliver the first pizza to the furthest location first— the customer is in the center of a U-shaped building. Web Zip through the trees when returning along the river to the pizza parlor.	550
8	3	349.3, 467.9, 555.1	1:25	Travel east and deliver the first pizza to the window washers on the scaffold. Wall Crawl beside them to make the delivery. The other customers are street-level.	600
9	3	377.8, 541.4, 616.7	1:45	Head south along the river before turning east for the first delivery to window washers on the ERDCO building. The second customer is suspended on scaffolding to the north, and the third is atop the container mover south of the pizza parlor.	650

MISSION #	# OF PIZZAS	DELIVERY DISTANCES	TIME LIMIT	NOTES	HERO POINTS EARNED
10	4	300.0, 395.2, 464.2, 647.2	1:25	Quickly Web Swing through the nearby park and then begin a wide counterclockwise loop. The first two customers are on scaffolding high off the ground, so be prepared to Wall Crawl to them. The other two are on the ground, so keep the jostling to a minimum during the descent.	700
11	4	329.2, 663.6, 912.0, 1136.7	1:55	Head north along the waterfront in a straight line. The first two deliveries are to guys on scaffolding, whereas the third and fourth are on the ground.	750
12	4	459.9, 571.1, 581.7, 679.3	1:40	Web Zip south along the water to the first delivery on the boat. Head to the hospital next, and then up to the window washers on the building with the skybridge. The fourth delivery is on the nearby rooftop.	800
13	4	605.0, 664.7, 855.1, 968.7	2:00	Head east toward the window washers first, and then loop around the south side of the large white building to make the second delivery. The final two deliveries are both on the street, on the way back to the pizza parlor.	850
14	4	603.9, 743.1, 772.3, 1057.7	1:55	Swing south to the customer near the warehouses via the smokestacks. Then head due east to the two customers at street level. Visit the fourth customer on the scaffold last.	900
15	4	332.7, 468.9, 930.0, 1332.7	1:55	Visit the window washers near the tanks first. Then head south to Chelsea Center. Swing out to the customer on the pier, and then make the final delivery on the way back to the pizza parlor.	950
16	5	229.1, 454.5, 937.0, 1014.9, 1061.1	2:20	Web Zip across the nearby park to the window washer. Continue south to Chelsea Center, and then turn east to the sports arena. Loop back to the northeast while dropping off the other pizzas along the way.	1000
17	5	598.6, 815.5, 826.3, 1301.7, 1332.7	2:05	Web Swing to the nearest customer, and then quickly cut east to the two customers across from one another. Head north to the next window washer customer. Then slip through the buildings on the campus to make the final delivery to the lady on the ground. Return along the waterfront and Web Zip across the water to the pizza parlor to shave a second off the end.	1050
18	5	441.0, 599.1, 633.4, 702.0, 867.9	1:45	Race to the east toward the tall black building for the first delivery. Then zigzag back and forth across the neon-lit avenue to make the next two deliveries. Swing through the alley to the window washer. Then Web Swing up and over the hospital to reach the customer on the sidewalk.	1100
19	6	511.6, 857.6, 876.3, 1009.1, 1047.6, 1421.4	3:00	Web Swing to the nearest customer first, and then head to the one inside the right-hand courtyard of the ornate building to the east. Weave through the skyscrapers and climb the tallest one to the east. Dive off the building and Web Swing to the upper ledge of the nearby black building. Visit the customer on the tall, angled building to the northwest. Then Web Zip through the trees to the middle of Central Park.	1150
20	6	209.9, 829.5, 981.3, 1088.9, 1164.5, 1295.6	2:25	Leap onto the buoy while holding the Grab Button to keep from slipping off. Now head across the park to the south, to the customer on the fire escape. Then visit the guy on the roof of the building with the two towers. Now loop around to the north while dropping off the pizzas on each of the other tall buildings.	1200

Photo Missions

Peter's other job is as a freelance photographer for the Daily Bugle. Although the Daily Bugle's publisher, Mr. Jameson, doesn't ever have any assignments for Peter, one of the editors by the name of Robbie does. Robbie helps out Peter by offering him an assignment during Chapter 4. From that point on, Peter can return to the Daily Bugle during his free time to ask Robbie for an assignment. Robbie seldom refuses.

Robbie "marks Peter's Map" by placing Camera Tokens where he wants the photos taken. Sprint to the restroom to exit the Daily Bugle as Spider-Man, and then follow the yellow Destination Marker to the first Camera Token. Move into position and press the Attack Button to take the photo. Spider-Man must race back to the Daily Bugle and reenter the building through the rooftop ventilation system. Hurry into the newsroom and bring the pictures to the secretary on the left so that she'll get Mr. Jameson's attention.

Photo Mission Data

MISSION #	TIME LIMIT	# OF PHOTOS	NOTES	HERO POINTS EARNED
1	2:30	5	Head a few blocks southwest and photograph the art gallery. Several of the Camera Tokens are on the street, but others are hovering above nearby buildings.	750
2	2:20	6	Swing northwest to the sports arena and take a series of photos of it from all sides. Most of the Camera Tokens are high up on nearby buildings, so remember to Wallsprint and leap upward to speed things up.	1000
3	2:35	7	Head northeast toward the library, while keeping the large skyscraper on the left. It's faster to swing around the subject building than it is to run and jump across its roof.	1250
4	3:50	9	Swing to the large construction site and photograph it from numerous angles. Spider-Man needs to take photos from above the vertical I-beams, atop the crane, and from within the elevator shaft.	1500
5	4:40	10	Head south toward the Financial District and take photos from many buildings there. The first six Camera Tokens are in close proximity to one another, but may require a moment to get your bearings. The final four Camera Tokens are strung out in a northward path across the roofs of four separate skyscrapers. Quickly swing back to the west to the busy avenue leading back to the Daily Bugle.	1750
6	4:14	11	Web Swing to the southeast corner of Central Park to the first Camera Token. The other eight Camera Tokens are aligned in a zigzag pattern that weaves back and forth through Central Park but also uses the rooftops of many nearby buildings. Try to Web Swing from the tallest trees to keep off the ground, and Web Zip whenever this isn't possible.	2000
7	4:20	12	Web Swing through Midtown to the super tall skyscraper, and climb up it to the first Camera Token. The second is just above very top of the spire and can be reached only by jumping from a Wall Crawl while holding the Sprint Button. The other Camera Tokens are much easier to reach; watch for the two on the sides of the oval building.	2250
8	4:25	13	Race to the Queensboro Bridge for a very thorough photo session. Spider-Man must take photos from above the bridge, from underneath it, and even from above a buoy in the water. This is a very difficult Photo Mission and it all comes down to your jumping accuracy. Also, remember that Spider-Man cannot jump while Wall Crawling upside down without falling.	2500

MISSION #	TIME LIMIT	# OF PHOTOS	NOTES	HERO POINTS EARNED
9	4:20	14	Navigating the elevated train track can prove to be quite a challenge. Several mid-air Camera Tokens make precision jumping a must. Feel free to take a moment to time your jumps; misjudging a tough jump can lead to a time-consuming fall. Web Swinging in the gap between the train tracks and adjacent buildings can make covering large distances easier.	2750
10	4:10	15	This is the king of all Photo Missions. Web swing through the tall buildings of Midtown, all the way to the Queensboro Bridge. Travel underneath the bridge with two or three web swings, using your last Web Swing to reach the first Camera Token. Reaching the first Camera Token with about 3:20 left on the clock will leave you in good shape for the rest of the mission. Use fully charged jumps and double jumps to reach the many midair and buoy Camera Tokens around the island. Develop a pattern for quickly snapping each photo, and the Shutterbug award will be yours.	3000

Mary Jane Missions

Spider-Man has to stop by Mary Jane's apartment (in Soho) in Chapter 6, and he finds a message on the door telling him to meet her at the movie theatre. From this point on, Spider-Man can drop by Mary Jane's apartment at any time to find a message telling him where to meet her. These very subtle side missions are known as the Mary Jane Missions and consist of racing to a single destination as fast as possible. Spider-Man needs to locate the Change Icon in the vicinity of each destination to change into Peter Parker before time expires. Complete all six of the Mary Jane Missions to earn the "Lover Not a Fighter" award.

SPEED FREAKS ONLY

The fifth and sixth Mary Jane Missions are incredibly difficult to pass without the Level 8 Swing Speed Upgrade. In fact, they're still quite difficult with the maximum upgrade, so don't spend too much time attempting them before fully upgraded.

Mary Jane Mission Data

MISSION #	TIME LIMIT	DISTANCE	MEETING PLACE	NOTES	HERO POINTS EARNED
1	0:40	363.5	Movie Theatre	Head north three blocks and then cut to the east to find the movie theatre. It's the blue building with the tall sign. The Change Icon is behind the theatre, near the dumpsters.	600
2	0:50	714.3	Restaurant	The restaurant is almost due east of Mary Jane's apartment. Web Swing along the avenues leading east, and jump up a block to the north whenever a building is in the way.	800
3	0:35	785.0	Boutique	Head north a few blocks. Then Web Swing onto the lower roof in the center of the multi-tiered brick building to reach the Change Icon.	1000
4	0:35	946.7	Theatre	This is a straight trip north via the main avenue. Watch for the "Y" and veer to the right. The Change Icon is in the alley behind the parked car.	1200
5	1:05	1930.3	Park	Spider-Man must race as quickly as possible to the small park near the pizza parlor on the Lower West Side. Head north past the Daily Bugle, and then cut west toward the arcade. The Change Icon is in the alley across from the park.	1400
6	1:02	2503.1	Museum	Mary Jane wants to meet with Peter at the Museum on the east side of Central Park. Cut over one street to the west and race uptown as fast and straight as possible. Veer to the right at the "Y" and slip through the narrow alley between the skyscrapers. Quickly wrap around the left side of the large building in front of the park, and race along the avenue to the museum.	1600

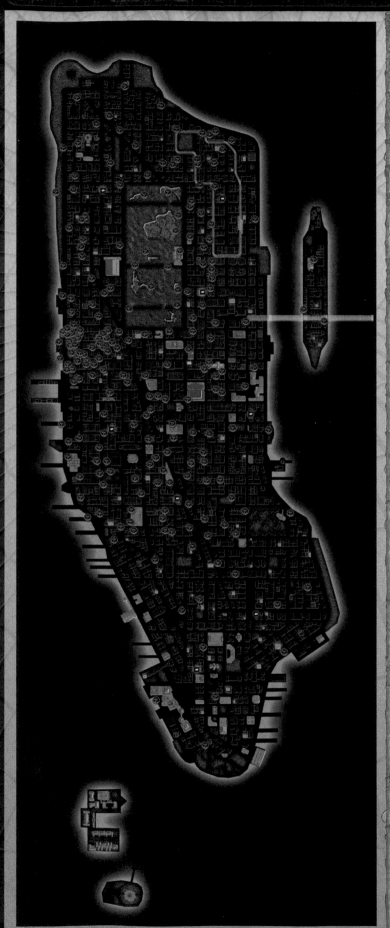

Hint Markers

Just because you have a superhero at your control, doesn't mean you won't need some tips from time to time. Fortunately, there are over 200 Hint Markers scattered throughout the city that can be accessed at any time. These bright green Hint Markers provide information that is usually helpful, sometimes trivial, and often comical. But best of all is the fact that each and every Hint Marker accessed nets Spider-Man at least 10 Hero Points the first time he encounters it.

This map shows the distribution of all 213 Hint Markers, most of which are very easily spotted on main city streets or on the ground in alleyways. Access the Zoom Map and scroll to the Hint Markers screen to see an in-game map of all the Hint Marker locations. Hint Markers that have already been accessed are shown with yellow circles around them on the Zoom Map to help Spider-Man avoid returning to the same one twice.

Challenge Tokens

When Peter Parker said that the city is Spider-Man's playground, he wasn't joking. There are 150 Challenge Tokens scattered throughout the city that serve as a way to test Spider-Man's acrobatic prowess. Each of these bright blue icons can be accessed whenever Spider-Man is not currently involved in a mission. Not only are they a lot of fun, but they are also a great source of Hero Points.

PRESS ⊗ TO ACCESS
RACE 54, DIFFICULTY: EASY
TYPE: WALLSPRINT, BEST TIME: 1:30.0

Challenges can be thought of as unique races that test Spider-Man's ability to reach key locations as quickly as possible. Each Challenge has a set goal time, and Spider-Man must reach the end of the course faster than the specified time in order to earn the Hero Points bonus. Once a Challenge has been completed, Spider-Man has the option of attempting to complete the "Mega" version of that Challenge. The racecourse doesn't change during a Mega Challenge, but the time requirement is far stiffer.

NEXT TRICK: WALLJUMP
TO WALLJUMP, PRESS Ⓐ WHILE WALL
SLIDING

Challenge Difficulties and Rewards

DIFFICULTY	NORMAL REWARD	MEGA REWARD
Easy	300	500
Medium	500	700
Hard	700	1000
Insane	1000	1500

View the Zoom Map and scroll over to the Challenges overlay to see a map of all of the Challenge Token locations. Challenge Tokens with a single yellow ring around them have been completed in their normal state, but only those with two yellow rings around them have had their Mega version completed.

Although the Challenges identified as "Easy" and "Medium" can be completed early in the game, the more difficult Challenges require numerous Swing Speed Upgrades to complete successfully. After several failed attempts on a particular Challenge, exit the Challenge by accessing the Pause Screen and give it another try after purchasing more Swing Speed Upgrades later in the game.

Many of the Challenges can be completed with skillful Web Swinging, but many others necessitate landing on the ground, Wallsprinting, Poleswinging, Wall Jumping, and performing specific tricks like Loops and Orbits.

Once a Challenge is initiated, a series of Trick Markers appears one by one throughout the city. Small yellow Destination Markers help show where the next marker is, if it's not in view. Each of these Trick Markers have specific illustrations on them to show what type of trick must be performed while Spider-Man passes through the marker. Spider-Man can expect to encounter the following Trick Markers during the Challenges:

GENERIC

This is the most common marker, and Spider-Man can pass through it doing any type of stunt or maneuver he wishes, but the basic Web Swing is usually be the best option.

CRAWLING

Spider-Man must pass through this marker while Wall Crawling in order to gain credit for reaching it. Swing or jump toward the wall and press the Grab Button to Wall Crawl. Hold the Sprint Button to ensure that Spider-Man is moving as fast as possible.

LAND

These markers appear on rooftops and on the street, and Spider-Man must be in contact with the ground when he reaches the marker. Note that he doesn't need to actually "land" on the marker—he can pass through it while running.

WALLSPRINT

Spider-Man must pass through the Trick Marker while Wallsprinting. Run and leap toward the wall near the marker, and hold the Sprint Button while pressing the Grab Button to make Spider-Man begin Wallsprinting. It's best to start the Wallsprint a few steps in front of the marker.

LOOP

This is one of the most difficult trick markers to clear, as it requires Spider-Man to pass through it while performing a loop on his Web Swing. Not only does this require precise Web Swinging and liberal use of the Sprint Button for generous Swing Boosts, but it also requires numerous Swing Speed Upgrades and considerable practice.

ORBIT

An Orbit is a special trick that involves Spider-Man swinging in a tight horizontal loop around a narrow object, such as the antenna atop a skyscraper or the spire of a cathedral. This is an advanced maneuver and should not be attempted without several Swing Speed upgrades.

POLE SWING

The Pole Swing marker is a rare occurrence, but Spider-Man must be ready for it when he sees it. Leap onto the flagpole or light pole that has the Pole Swing trick marker, and immediately press the Grab Button to begin the Pole Swing. Release the Grab Button to send Spider-Man flying through the air in the direction of the next Trick Marker.

WALL JUMP

The Wall Jump is a trick that is simple to perform, but difficult to completely master. Web Swing or Wallsprint into position above the Wall Jump Trick Marker, and then push against the wall to make Spider-Man Wall Slide down the side of the building. Press the Jump Button as he reaches the Trick Marker to perform the Wall Jump.

Challenge Data

CHALLENGE #	NEIGHBORHOOD	DIFFICULTY	TYPE	BEST TIME	# OF MARKERS	NOTES	MEGA TIME
1	Financial District	Easy	Race	5:00	10	This lengthy race zigzags north from the southern tip of the island all the way to the campus just south of Harlem. The key is to use the Web Zip to maintain elevation and momentum and to keep an eye on the Mini Map to avoid making the wrong turn.	4:00
2	Financial District	Easy	Race	5:00	10	This Web Swing race leads from the very southern tip of Manhattan all the way to the northernmost reaches of Harlem. The markers are widely spaced, and there is plenty of time to stick to the widest streets and to go around the taller buildings.	2:45
3	Financial District	Medium	Race	0:45	7	Sprint and jump from building to building to land on each of the markers. The first two markers and final two markers are each on the same building.	0:30
4	Financial District	Hard	Climbing	1:05	5	Carefully drop to the street and then race up the adjacent skyscraper. Repeat this one more time for the neighboring building, then leap and Web Zip to the final marker.	0:45
5	Financial District	Easy	Race	0:30	6	Sprint across the rooftop ledges in a tight circle to reach the markers. This race ends at the starting position and requires little jumping.	0:20
6	Financial District	Easy	Race	1:10	4	Wallsprint up the first building and then quickly drop back to the ground. Then race up the building across the street. Web Zip to the next skyscraper to finish.	0:35
7	Financial District	Medium	Race	1:10	8	This is a straightforward Web Swing race. Swing high when going into the final marker, as it sits atop the ledge of a building.	0:45
8	Financial District	Hard	Race	1:00	1	Spider-Man must race uptown to the upper reaches of one of the city's tallest skyscrapers. Use the wide avenue and make liberal use of the Sprint Button to gain as much Web Boost as possible.	0:50
9	Financial District	Medium	Race	1:50	1	Head north through the city to the upper reachess of New York City's second tallest skyscraper. Web Swing through the widest avenues to reach the building. Then use the Wallsprint to climb the skyscraper as fast as possible.	1:20
10	Financial District	Easy	Race	1:00	8	Web Swing northeast from the waterfront through the Civic Center area to Tribeca. Use the Web Zip to cross the park through the treetops.	0:30
11	Financial District	Medium	Race	1:20	8	This race features a very windy Web Swing portion in which all of the markers are close together. The final marker, however, is atop a skyscraper several blocks away. Don't start climbing until you check with the Mini Map to make sure you're on the right building.	0:45
12	Financial District	Insane	Race	1:20	10	Drop to the street and carefully leap to the buoy where the first marker is. Hold the Grab Button to prevent falling off. Follow the course through the Wallsprinting markers and Loop. Try to approach the Orbit markers fast and from the side. Watch the Mini Map to see where the next marker is before letting go.	1:05

CHALLENGE #	NEIGHBORHOOD	DIFFICULTY	TYPE	BEST TIME	# OF MARKERS	NOTES	MEGA TIME
13	Financial District	Medium	Race	1:00	9	Sprint and Web Zip from rooftop to rooftop to each of the markers. Spider-Man must touch down on each marker for it to count. The markers are primarily aligned in a straight path.	0:47
14	Financial District	Medium	Race	1:05	4	The race ends by the sports arena. Although it starts out straight, the route starts to zigzag through numerous side streets, so be ready for it.	0:45
15	Tribeca	Insane	Mixed	1:00	9	The first eight markers are all in the same general area, positioned across three buildings. Go back and forth between the roofs using the Orbits and Walljumps for momentum.	0:50
16	Tribeca	Insane	Race	0:55	10	This lengthy race features mostly alternating Walljump and Wallsprint markers, with one Loop marker in the middle of the race. The final marker requires Spider-Man to land on top of an antenna; charge the Jump Meter just over halfway to reach the right height.	0:40
17	Tribeca	Medium	Race	1:40	5	This is a lengthy race that forces Spider-Man to Web Swing through the mazelike streets of the Financial District. Check the Mini Map often to look for wider openings.	1:05
18	Tribeca	Easy	Race	1:10	10	Sprint across the rooftop to the markers. Use the Web Zip to propel Spider-Man across the street to the other rooftop and continue the sprint.	0:30
19	Tribeca	Hard	Race	0:45	10	The markers are all on the many ledges of this building. Check the Mini Map for the relative elevation of the marker. Then carefully run around the building to get it.	0:31
20	Civic Center	Hard	Race	0:55	8	Web Swing and Web Zip from roof to roof to reach the markers. The third, fourth, and fifth markers are all on the same building, so don't hastily leap from the roof.	0:50
21	Chinatown	Hard	Race	0:35	5	Web Swing around the course in a clockwise direction as fast as possible. Many of the streets are narrow so release from the Web Swing at the bottom of your arc to maintain a straight trajectory.	0:30
22	Chinatown	Insane	Mixed	0:35	10	The first eight markers are near the starting point. Spider-Man must Wallsprint and Walljump back and forth between both sides of this U-shaped building. The final two markers are further down the street.	0:25
23	Chinatown	Hard	Mixed	0:50	10	This race starts out with a lot of stylish Wallsprinting. The eighth marker requires Spider-Man to perform a Loop while Web Swinging from the corner of a building. The race then heads across two rooftops to the finish.	0:40
24	Lower East Side	Medium	Race	1:05	10	Charge the Jump Meter and make a series of running leaps from roof to roof to land on each of the markers. Remember to Web Zip if it looks like Spider-Man might come up short.	0:47
25	Lower East Side	Medium	Race	0:35	8	This lengthy Wall Crawling race takes some practice, but pausing to see where the next marker is will go a long way toward completing it. Hold the Sprint Button whenever crawling, and use the Walljump maneuver to leap to other buildings, as they're always across the street from one another.	0:20
26	Lower East Side	Hard	Race	0:30	9	Carefully drop onto the lower ledge of the building. Then sprint and dive in a clockwise direction around the ledge's perimeter to hit each of the first eight markers. Leap back to the roof to the final marker.	0:27

CHALLENGE #	NEIGHBORHOOD	DIFFICULTY	TYPE	BEST TIME	# OF MARKERS	NOTES	MEGA TIME
27	Lower East Side	Hard	Race	0:22	5	Zigzag through the alleys to the markers between some buildings and on others. Use the Web Zip to maintain the proper elevation, and be ready for sudden shifts in direction.	0:18
28	Lower East Side	Medium	Race	2:00	7	This is a lengthy race that covers a considerably wide area. Most of the markers are atop skyscrapers, so be sure to upgrade the Web Swing Speed and pause to identify the next marker's location before swinging wildly after it.	1:35
29	Soho	Medium	Race	0:45	8	This is a very twisty Web Swing race course. Be prepared to make sharp turns while Web Swinging in the early part of the race.	0:30
30	Soho	Easy	Race	1:30	7	Web Swing across the city to the Lower East Side. There is a turn at each marker, so be prepared for them.	0:45
31	Soho	Medium	Race	3:00	10	Each of the markers are high above the ground. Get to the highest point close by each marker, charge the Jump Meter, and then leap straight up toward it. Use the Web Zip to quickly double back to the high ground to avoid climbing buildings twice.	1:25
32	West Village	Medium	Race	1:10	8	Each of the markers require Spider-Man to touch down atop a different rooftop. Charge the Jump Meter, Sprint before leaping, and use the Web Zip to maintain elevation and avoid Wall Crawling.	0:50
33	West Village	Easy	Race	1:40	10	Web Zip and Web Swing through the markers en route to The Club. Each Marker is on the ground, so time your landings just right.	1:00
34	Greenwich Village	Easy	Race	1:10	1	Web Swing to the East Village while using the Swing Boost to go as fast as possible.	0:35
35	Greenwich Village	Insane	Mixed	0:40	9	This race consists of a lengthy lap around the block, but it incorporates strategically placed Walljump, Wallsprint, and Poleswing markers to help maintain Spider-Man's momentum. A lot can be learned about stylish locomotion by studying the placement of the markers on this course.	0:35
36	Greenwich Village	Medium	Race	0:30	4	Web Swing through the city to each of the markers. The final marker is pretty high off the ground, so use a really high Web Swing to elevate Spider-Man, and then Web Zip straight toward the marker.	0:15
37	Greenwich Village	Hard	Race	1:00	6	The markers for this Web Swinging race are all pretty high off the ground, so swing high into the air and use the Web Zip to maintain loft. The Web Zip also makes it possible to turn around midair and tag a missed marker.	0:50
38	Greenwich Village	Insane	Mixed	0:50	10	The first four markers require Spider-Man to Walljump on an angle in order to zigzag back and forth across the street to different buildings. So, have the Jump Meter charged. The race becomes slightly more straightforward after that, but it concludes with a lengthy Wallsprint with a Walljump marker positioned directly above it.	0:34
39	East Village	Hard	Race	2:20	9	This lengthy race incorporates some tricky Web Swinging through narrow streets, but also requires the occasional Wallsprint to the top of a skyscraper. Keep an eye on the Mini Map and expect the unexpected.	1:55
40	East Village	Medium	Race	1:30	9	Web Swing through the city in a large loop and return back to the race's starting point by touching down on the rooftop.	0:35

CHALLENGE #	NEIGHBORHOOD	DIFFICULTY	TYPE	BEST TIME	# OF MARKERS	NOTES	MEGA TIME
41	East Village	Medium	Race	1:05	6	This race has several lengthy straight-aways for fast Web Swinging, but beware that the final marker is on the ledge of a building right above the fifth marker.	0:45
42	East Village	Insane	Mixed	1:00	10	This race features many different markers but they all flow well into one another. Remember to Walljump off to the left to continue the clockwise trip around the area.	0:43
43	East Village	Hard	Race	1:00	8	Most of the markers hover high above the ground between buildings in this race. Fully charge the Jump Meter, hold the Sprint Button, and then take off through the air toward the marker.	0:35
44	East Village	Medium	Race	0:50	5	This is a straightforward race across a series of rooftops. Run and jump as far as possible, and use the Web Zip whenever Spider-Man is going to come up short.	0:35
45	Chelsea	Medium	Race	1:10	10	Use the Web Zip to help propel Spider-Man from rooftop to rooftop to complete this racecourse. Keep the Jump Meter charged and ready to launch Spider-Man off the edge of the buildings toward his next goal.	0:40
46	Chelsea	Insane	Mixed	1:05	10	Sprint and dive through the markers. Then rush toward the nearby building for a pair of Walls prints. Maintain momentum through the two Walljumps. Then Web Swing for several blocks to reach the next two markers. Spider-Man must land on top of the horseman statue in the park to finish the race.	0:47
47	Chelsea	Medium	Race	0:45	10	This is a lengthy race involving a lot of Web Swinging. Be prepared to make frequent turns in the middle of the race. Also, try to swing high and leap onto the building at the finish to reach the final marker.	0:30
48	Chelsea	Medium	Race	0:45	5	This is a great Challenge to see how fast you get Spider-Man going with his Web Swing. It's a straight shot through the first four markers and then a Wallsprint up the building where the final marker is.	0:24
49	Chelsea	Hard	Race	0:45	3	This is a difficult Web Swing race that requires Spider-Man to navigate a narrow street with many buildings angled off to the sides. Leap from each Web Swing at the bottom of the arc to maintain momentum. Alternate sides of the street to avoid getting pulled into an alley.	0:40
50	Chelsea	Hard	Walljump	0:30	9	Wallsprint up the wall and start to Wall Slide back down to the marker. Charge the Jump Meter at least halfway before performing the Walljump to reach the next marker. Once at the top of this "valley," Web Zip over the nearby buildings to the next two markers.	0:27
51	Chelsea	Hard	Race	0:21	1	Dive off the roof and Web Swing on an angle to the left to line up Spider-Man with the wide avenue leading to the marker. Take lengthy swings to get Spider-Man aloft, then Wallsprint and leap toward the marker.	0:18
52	Flat Iron	Easy	Race	2:00	8	Web Swing a lengthy clockwise loop past the Daily Bugle and New York's tallest skyscraper.	0:45
53	Flat Iron	Medium	Climbing	1:00	4	Race up and down two nearby buildings, then leap and swing across to the final marker on another building.	0:35

CHALLENGE #	NEIGHBORHOOD	DIFFICULTY	TYPE	BEST TIME	# OF MARKERS	NOTES	MEGA TIME
54	Flat Iron Village	Easy	Wallsprint	1:30	6	Be sure to hold the Sprint Button before jumping onto the wall and pressing the Grab Button, else Spider-Man won't Wallsprint.	0:25
55	Flat Iron	Medium	Race	0:45	1	This is a race against the clock to reach the helipad atop the black skyscraper in the distance. Web Swing up and over the shorter buildings, and then Wallsprint up the skyscraper as fast as possible.	0:30
56	Flat Iron	Medium	Race	1:30	6	This race is purely Web Swinging but each of the markers gets progressively higher off the ground. Hold onto the Web Line longer and longer before jumping off.	0:45
57	Gramercy	Hard	Race	0:40	9	Web Swing through the city as fast as possible to make this short time limit. The final marker is atop a ledge on a building and requires two sharp turns to reach it.	0:35
58	Gramercy	Medium	Race	1:00	7	Web Swing in a zigzag fashion through the nearby city blocks. Then Wallsprint up the building with the "Bortolux" sign on it to the finish.	0:35
59	Gramercy	Hard	Race	0:50	9	Keep charging the Jump Meter and holding the Sprint Button to have Spider-Man fling himself through the air from rooftop to rooftop. Be prepared for sudden changes in direction, and Web Zip when necessary to make the lengthier leaps. Double jumps come in handy during this race.	0:45
60	Gramercy	Medium	Race	1:00	6	Wallsprint up and down the buildings as fast as possible while charging the Jump Meter to get a boost. Drop off the buildings to the street as fast as possible.	0:35
61	Gramercy	Hard	Mixed	0:55	7	This race features an exciting mix of Walljump and Wallsprint markers that are placed to help keep Spider-Man's momentum going around corners. Keep the Jump Meter charged when Wallsprinting, and be ready to Wall Slide whenever a red marker appears.	0:25
62	Garment District	Insane	Mixed	0:40	10	This race features a number of Walljumps that require some practice before mastering. When performing the Loop at the ninth marker, be sure to land back on the rooftop next to that marker, as the final marker rests atop the antenna.	0:30
63	Garment District	Medium	Race	1:00	5	Web Zip and jump from rooftop to rooftop. The markers start out leading away from the start but then double back, so pay close attention to the Destination Marker and the Mini Map to prevent rushing off in the wrong direction.	0:26
64	Garment District	Hard	Race	0:09	1	Charge the Jump Meter and leap into a vertical Wallsprint up the side of the building. Leap a second time and continue Wallsprinting to the lone marker on the roof.	0:05
65	Garment District	Medium	Race	1:20	9	Race up to the roof of the adjacent building and begin crossing the city from rooftop to rooftop. Use the Web Zip to maintain elevation, and keep the Jump Meter charged and ready for a long distance jump at all times.	0:55
66	Garment District	Easy	Race	0:40	4	Web Swing around the block in a clockwise direction as fast as possible.	0:10

CHALLENGE #	NEIGHBORHOOD	DIFFICULTY	TYPE	BEST TIME	# OF MARKERS	NOTES	MEGA TIME
67	Garment District	Hard	Wallsprint	0:35	7	This lengthy race has multiple markers on the left side of the street. They are spaced fairly far apart, so charge the Jump Meter while Wallsprinting. Be ready to turn to the left and switch to the right-hand side of the street for the final stretch.	0:26
68	Garment District	Hard	Mixed	1:10	5	The trick to this race is not wasting too much time on the second marker. Spider-Man must drop off the side of the building, attach a very short Web Line to the corner of the roof, and swing in a Loop through the marker. Continue past the other markers and then to the top of the skyscraper.	0:50
69	Garment District	Easy	Race	0:30	5	Web Swing and Web Zip to the arcade northwest of the starting point. Dive off the first building and gradually descend. Spider-Man must touch the ground at the final marker.	0:08
70	Midtown	Easy	Race	1:45	6	Race up the side of the adjacent building, and prepare for a lengthy figure eight Web Swing trip to the Theatre District.	0:50
71	Midtown	Medium	Race	0:45	3	Dive off the skyscraper and Web Zip through the first marker and onto the nearby rooftop. Carefully plummet to the final marker on the street below.	0:15
72	Midtown	Medium	Race	0:45	5	The first four markers alternate between being on the ground and in the air. The final marker is atop a nearby building.	0:22
73	Midtown	Medium	Climbing	1:20	4	Race up and down two skyscrapers, and then Web Swing over to the tallest skyscraper in this part of New York City. Wallsprint as fast as possible to the top of its needle.	0:55
74	Midtown	Hard	Race	0:40	5	Wallsprint up the building near the start, and launch into the air for the first marker. The next three markers are high in the air and require that Spider-Man not jump from his Web Swing until high in his arc.	0:22
75	Midtown	Medium	Race	0:50	3	This is a very straightforward Web Swing race designed to see how fast Spider-Man can go. There is only one turn, but the buildings angle away from the road, so alternate sides of the road when swinging.	0:30
76	Midtown	Insane	Mixed	1:15	10	This race covers a lot of ground, and it's important for Spider-Man to pause and see where the next marker is before rushing off. It's also very important that Spider-Man Wall Slide down the sides of the skyscrapers to avoid freefalling to his death.	0:58
77	Midtown	Medium	Race	0:30	4	Leap across the rooftops of the nearby buildings as fast as possible. Then hurl Spider-Man toward the cathedral, and Web Zip to the final marker hovering between the two spires.	0:14
78	Midtown	Hard	Race	0:55	10	This entire race takes place on the buildings just south of Central Park. Make calculated jumps to land on each of the ornate white building's circular towers. Be sure not to charge the Jump Meter when performing the Walljumps. Use the Web Zip to help Spider-Man reach the eighth marker floating high above the ground.	0:38
79	Midtown	Medium	Orbit	0:30	1	Wallsprint up the nearby building and Walljump toward the spire atop the cathedral. Web Swing around it in a circle to complete the orbit.	0:11

CHALLENGE #	NEIGHBORHOOD	DIFFICULTY	TYPE	BEST TIME	# OF MARKERS	NOTES	MEGA TIME
80	Midtown	Insane	Race	1:35	10	This long-distance race features many Wallsprint markers, but this time they force Spider-Man to climb skyscrapers. Be ready to alternate between delicately balancing on skyscraper ledges or antennas and vertical Wallsprinting. Remember to always tap the Grab Button to initiate a Wall Crawl after reaching a marker to avoid running in the wrong direction.	1:20
81	Midtown	Easy	Race	2:00	1	This race features just one marker. Dive off the skyscraper, and Web Swing and Web Zip due south to the building with the marker on it. Wallsprint up the side of the building to the finish.	0:45
82	Midtown	Easy	Race	1:40	5	Web Swing across town to the arcade. Be prepared to make quick snap-turns into narrow alleys.	0:30
83	Tudor City	Medium	Race	1:00	8	Web Swing and Web Zip through the city along this course. The third marker is high off the ground, so swing high before jumping. Use the Web Zip to tackle the markers on the ground.	0:30
84	Tudor City	Insane	Mixed	1:05	10	Use the two initial Poleswings to gain speed, and Walljump directly into the Orbit. The key to this race is picking up enough speed during the Orbit to fly through the marker that follows it. This marker is otherwise extremely hard to reach. Spider-Man should be able to fly from the Orbit through both generic markers with little more than a single Web Zip.	0:53
85	Tudor City	Medium	Race	0:50	1	Web Swing north through the city as fast as possible to the roof of the large museum near Central Park. Web Zip over the shorter buildings whenever possible to maintain a straight line.	0:35
86	Tudor City	Insane	Race	1:15	10	The middle section of this race features two Orbits and a Loop and is definitely the linchpin for this course. Approach the Orbit markers from the side, and shoot a moderately long Web Line to obtain a nearly horizontal swing arc. Use a short Web Line attached to the corner of the building when trying to perform the Loop. Try to flip Spider-Man up and onto the roof.	1:00
87	Tudor City	Medium	Race	0:50	8	This race begins with several markers resting on the ledge of the building. Then it quickly turns into a long distance Web Swing race from rooftop to rooftop.	0:40
88	Tudor City	Medium	Climbing	2:00	7	Race up and down multiple nearby skyscrapers. Wallsprint straight up each building while charging the Jump Meter. Then leap but quickly return to the Wallsprint to maintain momentum.	1:15
89	Tudor City	Hard	Race	1:25	8	Race across the Queensboro Bridge by Web Swinging through the upper portions of the support towers. Perform a Loop at the far end of the bridge, and then return along the same path. The final two markers are stacked on top of each other, so be ready for it.	1:10
90	Tudor City	Hard	Race	0:32	2	This is a drag race for Spider-Man to see how fast he can Web Swing the length of the Queensboro Bridge. Web Swing as fast as possible under the bridge to the first marker, bounce off the limit of the map ("Area Unavailable" will appear), and then return to the starting point.	0:27

CHALLENGE #	NEIGHBORHOOD	DIFFICULTY	TYPE	BEST TIME	# OF MARKERS	NOTES	MEGA TIME
91	Theatre District	Easy	Race	2:00	7	The final marker is very high up on a skyscraper, unlike the first six, which were only several stories above the ground.	0:45
92	Theatre District	Medium	Race	0:50	8	Run and leap to the markers on a series of rooftops. The jumps vary in distance, so don't always charge the Jump Meter, as the resulting hang time will only waste time.	0:35
93	Theatre District	Medium	Climbing	1:10	4	This is a short climbing race that forces Spider-Man to race up and down a couple nearby buildings. Race to the top of the final skyscraper, and then jump as high as possible to reach the marker above the building.	0:42
94	Theatre District	Hard	Race	0:55	6	Dive off the skyscraper and Web Swing through the city as fast as possible. The final marker is on a rooftop near the river, so be ready to Wallsprint up to it.	0:40
95	Lower West Side	Easy	Race	1:00	5	Wallsprint across the markers in the alleys. Be prepared to leap off of one wall and continue the Wallsprint on the opposing building.	0:15
96	Lower West Side	Easy	Race	0:20	3	Use the Web Zip and Web Swing techniques to make a quick counterclockwise loop around the small park.	0:10
97	Lower West Side	Easy	Race	1:00	3	Web Swing to the arcade in the nearby alley.	0:10
98	Lower West Side	Easy	Race	1:00	6	Web Swing through the bright lights of New York City as fast as possible.	0:15
99	Lower West Side	Easy	Poleswing	0:30	2	Fully charge the Jump Meter, leap across the street to the flagpole, and Poleswing to the right. Leap from the pole and grab the second one to the right (use the Web Zip if necessary).	0:06
100	Lower West Side	Medium	Race	1:10	10	This is a lengthy Web Swing race with markers that are pretty widely spaced. Hug the buildings close near the waterfront to maintain elevation.	0:50
101	Lower West Side	Medium	Race	0:20	4	Quickly jump from rooftop to rooftop to reach the markers. The fourth one will require a lengthy Web Zip to reach, so be ready.	0:14
102	Lower West Side	Insane	Mixed	0:38	10	Hop from awning to awning for the first two markers, and then prepare to alternate between Poleswinging and Wallsprinting for the next four markers. The race then moves to the rooftops for some extended racing.	0:26
103	Lower West Side	Easy	Race	2:00	7	Web Swing through the side streets, and then up and over the building to the alley behind it. There is a sharp turn at nearly every marker, so be prepared.	0:27
104	Central Park	Hard	Race	3:10	8	This difficult race requires the Level 8 Swing Speed Upgrade, as Spider-Man must make leap from his Web Swing and carry the entire lake in the center of the park. Race back and forth across the length of the park twice to complete this race. Look to Web Swing from any nearby helicopters to ensure that Spider-Man doesn't end up all wet.	2:50
105	Central Park	Hard	Mixed	0:55	10	Hit each of the markers atop the lampposts, and then Web Swing to the building. Reenter the park, and launch high into the air over the pond to reach the next marker. Be ready to land atop the "platform" marker. Then Web Swing and Web Zip through the remaining markers to complete this very difficult race.	0:38

CHALLENGE #	NEIGHBORHOOD	DIFFICULTY	TYPE	BEST TIME	# OF MARKERS	NOTES	MEGA TIME
106	Central Park	Hard	Race	1:15	7	Web Swing from the tallest trees to reach the markers without the risk of touching the ground. To save time, swing from the buildings across the street from the park when going for the third and fourth markers.	1:10
107	Central Park	Insane	Mixed	1:00	10	There are several tricky aspects of this race. For starters, Spider-Man must Walljump off a tree. To do so, hop against the tree while pushing toward it, and then quickly press the Jump Button. The hardest part of the course is the two high-altitude markers. If unable to hit both of them in one leap from a tree, try swinging from the building across the street. Lastly, Orbit around the tree, and let Spider-Man fly over the small pond to the finish.	0:48
108	Upper West Side	Medium	Race	0:25	5	Hold the Sprint Button and run through the markers. Use a Web Zip to reach the final Marker faster.	0:15
109	Upper West Side	Easy	Race	0:30	3	Web Swing along the avenue in a relatively straight line to complete this challenge with little trouble.	0:12
110	Upper West Side	Easy	Race	1:00	1	Web Swing south along the main avenue, and then cut through the alley to the west toward the arcade.	0:18
111	Upper West Side	Medium	Race	0:30	10	Each marker appears adjacent to the same building. Web Swing around the upper reaches of this building in an orbiting fashion to hit them all.	0:13
112	Upper West Side	Hard	Race	0:45	8	Swing through the trees of Central Park in a clockwise direction around the northern pond, and return to the starting point. Swing from the tallest trees and keep the Web Line short to avoid touching down.	0:40
113	Upper East Side	Medium	Race	1:35	9	Web Swing north and then circle back around to the east under the train tracks. Then head south to the United Nations building. Web Zip under the tracks and over the Queensboro Bridge to prevent getting hung up.	1:20
114	Upper East Side	Medium	Walljump	0:30	2	Wallsprint up the adjacent building, and quickly Walljump across the tracks to the marker on the roof.	0:04
115	Upper East Side	Medium	Race	1:25	8	Web Swing in a looping pattern around the Upper East Side and El Barrio. Stick close to the buildings near Central Park to avoid descending to the street.	0:55
116	Upper East Side	Medium	Climbing	1:05	7	Wallsprint up four buildings as fast as possible. Charge the Jump Meter to get a climbing boost, but immediately go back to the Wallsprint to maintain momentum.	0:50
117	Upper East Side	Medium	Platform	1:20	7	Fully charge the Jump Meter and leap from platform to platform across Central Park to the building on the other side. The second to last platform is very high, so don't hesitate to use a Web Zip to help Spider-Man reach it.	0:25
118	Upper East Side	Medium	Race	1:00	10	Sprint and leap as far as possible from roof to roof to land on each of the markers. Pay attention to the Mini Map, and don't leap until fully aware of the next marker's location.	0:50

CHALLENGE #	NEIGHBORHOOD	DIFFICULTY	TYPE	BEST TIME	# OF MARKERS	NOTES	MEGA TIME
119	Upper East Side	Insane	Wallsprint	0:54	9	Scale the upper reaches of the nearby buildings, and then begin Wallsprinting across the face of the buildings that flank the train tracks. Charge the Jump Meter to make the leap across the tracks to the next target. Wallsprint up toward the eighth marker on an angle to the right while charging the Jump Meter. Rocket Spider-Man into the air to reach the finish high above the ground.	0:37
120	Morningside	Hard	Wallsprint	0:45	6	Each marker is on the opposite side of the street of the one preceding it. Keep the Jump Meter charged and leap back and forth across the street to continue Wallsprinting.	0:25
121	Morningside	Medium	Race	0:45	6	Web Swing through the narrow alleys in as straight a line as possible. Watch out for the sudden turns, and release from the Web Swing at the bottom of the arc to maintain the proper direction.	0:30
122	Morningside	Medium	Race	0:45	3	The three markers are each positioned high in the sky above a different building. Wallsprint up the side of the building while charging the Jump Meter, and let fly off the highest point of the building to reach them.	0:25
123	Morningside	Medium	Race	0:40	5	This race takes place entirely on the campus. Leap and Web Zip from rooftop to rooftop as fast as possible.	0:25
124	Morningside	Medium	Race	0:45	10	The markers are spread across three nearby rooftops and the streets between them. Drop carefully off the ledges of each building, as many markers are directly below.	0:35
125	Morningside	Easy	Race	0:20	10	This is a jumping and running race that takes place entirely on this grassy park. This one takes some practice to know where and when to jump; it's not as easy as its difficulty rating suggests.	0:15
126	El Barrio	Medium	Race	0:50	10	Weave in and out through the narrow alleys of El Barrio while Web Swinging as fast as possible to the final marker. Use the Web Zip to stay aloft over the train tracks.	0:35
127	El Barrio	Medium	Race	2:20	10	This lengthy race is a test to see how fast Spider-Man can complete a lap around the train tracks. Web Zip and use the buildings to Web Swing to reach the markers faster. Be sure to cut off the northwest section of the track between the fourth and fifth markers.	1:35
128	El Barrio	Hard	Race	0:15	1	Sprint while charging the Jump Meter, and then leap down the tracks toward the marker. Charge the Jump Meter while airborne and release it just as Spider-Man touches down to Double Jump.	0:12
129	El Barrio	Medium	Wallsprint	0:40	6	Wallsprint across six of the support posts for the elevated train. Run and hop toward each of the markers, and then quickly press the Sprint and Grab Buttons to Wallsprint one or two steps across the post.	0:26
130	El Barrio	Hard	Race	0:15	4	Sprint and leap from rooftop to rooftop to reach the first two markers. Then quickly scamper up the wall to the third marker, and turn and leap to the left to the finish.	0:10
131	El Barrio	Medium	Race	0:50	8	This race zigzags through many city blocks as it heads south toward Central Park. Be extra careful not to get hung up on the elevated train tracks; consider Web Zipping under the tracks in a straight line.	0:30

CHALLENGE #	NEIGHBORHOOD	DIFFICULTY	TYPE	BEST TIME	# OF MARKERS	NOTES	MEGA TIME
132	El Barrio	Hard	Wallsprint	0:50	8	Hop into a Wallsprint and follow the markers around the block by Wallsprinting across the faces of the many buildings. Use a Web Zip to close on the further markers without losing momentum.	0:35
133	El Barrio	Medium	Race	1:30	1	This is a race to the ledge on the building facing the large cathedral. Web Swing south through the city as fast as possible, and then Wallsprint up the building to the lone marker.	1:00
134	El Barrio	Medium	Race	1:00	6	Race south toward Central Park while weaving through city streets and under the train tracks.	0:35
135	Manhattan Village	Medium	Race	1:00	7	This is a standard Web Swing race across town, ending with a marker atop a building near the waterfront.	0:45
136	Manhattan Village	Medium	Race	1:10	9	This lengthy Web Swing race goes through numerous narrow alleys, but also follows the underside of the elevated train tracks. Consider using the Web Zip maneuver to better follow a straight path.	0:40
137	Harlem	Hard	Wallsprint	0:35	7	Wallsprint down the street along the sides of the buildings, then turn around and come back on the opposite side. There are five markers on the way out, and then two more on the on the other side of the street leading back to the start.	0:30
138	Harlem	Hard	Walljump	0:20	10	Gradually climb the buildings by Walljumping back and forth across the street. Press the Jump Button while Wall Sliding over the marker to get credit for the Walljump.	0:15
139	Harlem	Hard	Race	0:35	6	Web Swing as fast as possible around the nearby blocks. Then race back up the side of the building to finish near the starting point.	0:31
140	Harlem	Medium	Race	0:30	8	Web Swing through the narrow alleyways between the buildings. Be ready to make numerous blind turns.	0:25
141	Harlem	Hard	Race	1:05	9	This lengthy race requires a good mix of long distance jumping and Web Swinging. Keep an eye on the Mini Map, and try to jump to nearby markers whenever possible.	0:57
142	Harlem	Medium	Race	5:30	4	This is an extremely long Web Swing race that leads Spider-Man on a zigzag path to the southern tip of the city. Keep an eye on the Mini Map, and try to stay near tall buildings to avoid touching down on the ground until the final marker.	4:00
143	Harlem	Hard	Mixed	1:10	10	Web Zip toward the crane to get momentum for the Loop. Then speed off on the clockwise loop around the nearby city blocks. Watch for the Poleswing and Wallsprint markers. Maintain momentum off the second Loop to finish fast toward the final marker.	1:00
144	Roosevelt Island	Hard	Race	0:35	1	Run and leap to the right, and Web Swing north along Roosevelt Island's eastern edge to avoid the obstacles in the island's center.	0:30
145	Roosevelt Island	Hard	Race	2:10	9	Race in a zigzag pattern along the suspension beams of the Queensboro Bridge. Charge the Jump Meter two-thirds full, and leap on an angle from one side to the other. Hold the Grab Button to keep from falling off.	0:55

CHALLENGE #	NEIGHBORHOOD	DIFFICULTY	TYPE	BEST TIME	# OF MARKERS	NOTES	MEGA TIME
146	Roosevelt Island	Insane	Mixed	0:40	10	This is a very difficult race requiring numerous Wallsprints and Poleswings. The beginning is the hardest part, as the path is less clear.	0:35
147	Roosevelt Island	Medium	Race	1:20	5	Race south along the west edge of the island. Then veer directly west under the Queensboro Bridge and toward the center of Central Park.	0:55
148	Ellis Island	Hard	Race	0:43	9	This race wraps around the entire island in a clockwise direction from rooftop to rooftop. Hold the Sprint Button and jump and Web Zip as far as possible to clear the larger distances.	0:38
149	Ellis Island	Hard	Mixed	0:40	7	Wallsprint around and out of the area near the start. Then Web Swing around the water tower and over to the flagpole. Orbit the flagpole, and then race back across the buildings to the center of the island.	0:35
150	Liberty Island	Hard	Race	0:30	1	The lone marker is atop the Statue of Liberty's raised torch. Use the Slingshot Jump and some quick Wall Crawling to reach it. Consider Web Swinging high into the air near the torch, and then let go and Web Zip onto the torch.	0:23

Exploration Tokens

There are hundreds of tokens scattered throughout the game for those players seeking total mastery. Keep an eye out for these black and gold tokens. Try to collect them all, as each one gives Spider-Man some additional Hero Points. Also, the only way to gain every award in the game is to seek out every one of these tokens.

SECRET TOKENS

Secret Tokens are the most difficult to find, as they are hidden well off the beaten path. Many of these tokens can be found on fire escapes, in back alleys, behind signs, and in many other hard-to-see places. There is a total of 75 Secret Tokens, each of which nets Spider-Man a minimum of 250 Hero Points.

The accompanying map shows the numbered locations of all 75 Secret Tokens. The numbers correspond to the information in the following table. Be sure to read the notes and look at the corresponding screenshot carefully, as many of the Secret Tokens can be quite difficult to find.

Secret Tokens

TOKEN #	NEIGHBORHOOD	NOTES	
1	Financial District	In the back of the large building, hovering above the water, near the walkways under the building.	
2	Financial District	In the small plaza in the center of the ring-like building.	
3	Financial District	On the tiny corner ledge of the building across from the grass.	
4	Financial District	Near the large glass dome in the center of the building near the waterfront.	
5	Financial District	On a lower portion of the large building, near the windows.	
6	Financial District	Behind one of the stone columns at the base of the building, up off the ground.	
7	Financial District	Behind one of the columns on the building's elevated base.	
8	Financial District	On the underside of the skybridge, where it connects to the building to the west.	
9	Financial District	Halfway up the red brick building in the alley.	

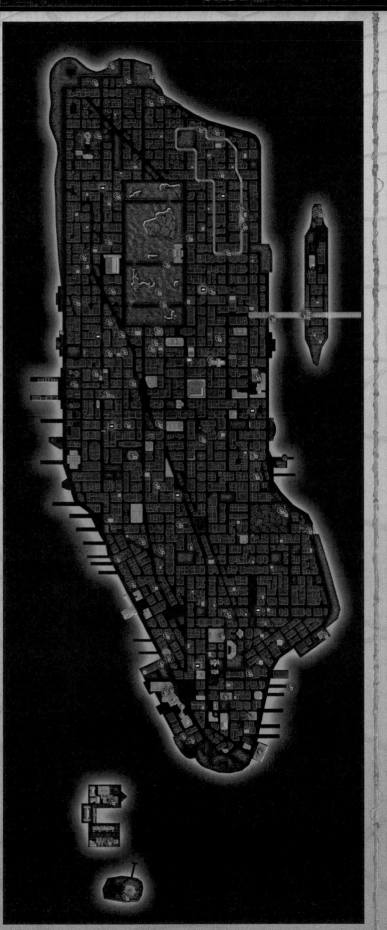

TOKEN #	NEIGHBORHOOD	NOTES	
10	Chinatown	In an alley near a red brick building.	
11	Financial District	Just above the water, on the far side of the pier.	
12	Tribeca	In the northwest corner of the warehouse property.	
13	Chinatown	Atop the roof of the theatre where Mysterio meets the reporters.	
14	Soho	On the apartment building's fire escape, one flight down from the top.	
15	Lower East Side	Under the factory's ventilation ductwork, on the side near the water.	
16	West Village	Between the two brick warehouses near the waterfront.	
17	West Village	In the corner of the alley, between two very tightly spaced buildings	
18	West Village	On the lower of the rooftops, in the corner behind the ventilation ducts.	
19	West Village	On the middle, second-story balcony of the tall red building.	
20	Greenwich Village	On the underside of the arch in the building.	
21	Gramercy	Atop the elevator shaft of the building under construction near the university.	
22	Gramercy	At the bottom of the elevator shaft of the building under construction.	
23	Gramercy	On the wall above the windows in the alley.	
24	Gramercy	On the east side of the fancy brick house, on the hidden balcony.	

TOKEN #	NEIGHBORHOOD	NOTES	
25	Flat Iron	On the south side of the building, several stories off the ground.	
26	Flat Iron	In the center of the sports arena's roof.	
27	Garment District	On the sidewalk between the landscaping and building.	
28	Midtown	On the roof, behind the large billboard.	
29	Midtown	Behind the ductwork atop the roof of the building.	
30	Tudor City	On the ground, on the north side of the large complex of buildings.	
31	Midtown	Hovering above the ground in the northwest corner of the cathedral.	
32	Midtown	On the ground in the small plaza in the center of the ring-shaped building.	
33	Tudor City	On the platform near the top of the westernmost tower of the Queensboro Bridge.	
34	Theatre District	On the roof of the hospital, behind the large red sign.	
35	Theatre District	In the triangular alley between the buildings.	
36	Lower West Side	Between the stacks of shipping containers in the cargo yard.	
37	Lower West Side	On the roof, between the ventilation ducts.	
38	Lower West Side	In the back of the alley between the buildings.	
39	Theatre District	In the back corner of the alley, behind the buildings.	

TOKEN #	NEIGHBORHOOD	NOTES	
40	Theatre District	In the alley between the buildings; drop off the rooftop to reach it.	
41	Theatre District	On the fire escape, three flights down from the top.	
42	Theatre District	In a small alcove in the center of the U-shaped building, on the ground.	
43	Lower West Side	On the corner ledge of the building directly above the busy avenue.	
44	Lower West Side	In the narrow alley behind the building.	
45	Lower West Side	In the square plaza in the center of the building complex, on the ground.	
46	Lower West Side	On the ground in the back corner of the alley.	
47	Upper West Side	On the ledge of the west side of the building.	
48	Upper West Side	In the narrow alley on the south side of the building.	
49	Upper East Side	Hovering above the ground in the very narrow slot in the building's southwest side.	
50	Central Park	On the roof of the tunnel in the southeast corner of the park.	
51	Central Park	In the tree on the small ridge southeast of the pond.	
52	Central Park	On the roof of the tunnel near the art museum.	
53	Upper East Side	On the east side of the curvy white museum.	
54	Upper East Side	Underneath the tracks for the elevated train, high off the ground.	

TOKEN #	NEIGHBORHOOD	NOTES	
55	El Barrio	Under the stairs leading up to the elevated train.	
56	El Barrio	High off the ground, just underneath the tracks for the elevated train.	
57	El Barrio	Underneath the building with the sky bridge, high above the ground.	
58	El Barrio	Atop the elevated train tracks, near a gap in the railing.	
59	El Barrio	Next to the dumpster in the alley between the buildings.	
60	Roosevelt Island	On the lower platform of the Queensboro Bridge's middle tower.	
61	Roosevelt Island	Hovering above the southern spire on the Queensboro Bridge's middle tower.	
62	Roosevelt Island	Hovering between the large blue smokestacks at the north end of the island.	
63	Upper West Side	On the grassy patch of land in the center of the ring-shaped building.	
64	Morningside	On the ledge of the building with a dome in the northeast corner of the campus.	
65	Harlem	In the alley, off the ground in the corner.	
66	Harlem	On the ledge of the lower roof, overlooking the grass near the water.	
67	Harlem	On the stack of containers near the shipping yard.	
68	Harlem	On the stack of containers near the eastern shipping yard.	
69	Harlem	Near a tree on the grassy field near the north end of the island.	

TOKEN #	NEIGHBORHOOD	NOTES	
70	Harlem	On the sidewalk between the river and grassy hill.	
71	Liberty Island	On the grass near the Statue of Liberty's large stone base.	
72	Ellis Island	On the roof of the large building on the north side of the island.	
73	Ellis Island	On the grass on the south side of the island, next to the large building.	
74	East Village	On the rooftop, in the northeastern corner of the building.	
75	Roosevelt Island	On the underside of the stone bridge tower on the west side of the island.	

HIDEOUT TOKENS

HIDEOUT

New York City is loaded with street gangs, thugs, and quite a few groups of experienced criminals. When not on the streets harassing the city's innocent people, these evildoers often lie low in one of their many hideouts. These hideouts are shaded red on the Mini Map and represent buildings that Spider-Man can enter.

There are a total of 37 hideouts, with each containing a Hideout Token worth 250 Hero Points. The majority of the hideouts are exercise gyms, bars, dance clubs, and restaurants, but some gangs choose to use abandoned apartments or basements as their home base. Keep an eye peeled for conspicuous doors or even open windows near fire escapes.

Spider-Man must be on alert when entering a hideout, as there is always a good chance that the local gang is there when Spider-Man arrives. Sometimes Spider-Man will find the hideout empty, and all he has to do is grab the Hideout Token. But other times there may be a gang of thugs looking to take Spider-Man out. Since there can be as many as three to eight thugs ready to rumble, Spider-Man shouldn't ever enter a hideout with less than half of his health.

The accompanying map shows all 37 Hideout Token locations. Each location has been numbered and corresponds to the location data and screenshot provided below.

TOKEN #	NEIGHBORHOOD	STOREFRONT	
1	Financial District	Exercise Gym	
2	Financial District	Bar	
3	Financial District	Bar	
4	Tribeca	Warehouse	
5	Tribeca	Building Basement	
6	Lower East Side	Dance Club	
7	Lower East Side	Exercise Gym	
8	Lower East Side	Bar	
9	Lower East Side	Dance Club	
10	West Village	Dance Club	
11	Greenwich Village	Abandoned Apartment	
12	Gramercy	Abandoned Building	

TOKEN #	NEIGHBORHOOD	STOREFRONT	
13	Flat Iron	Bar	
14	Chelsea	Warehouse	
15	Flat Iron	Building Basement	
16	Gramercy	Bar	
17	Gramercy	Bar	
18	Tudor City	Restaurant	
19	Midtown	Bar	
20	Tudor City	Warehouse	
21	Roosevelt Island	Abandoned Building	
22	Roosevelt Island	Bar	
23	Upper East Side	Restaurant	
24	Upper East Side	Dance Club	
25	Lower West Side	Bar	
26	Upper West Side	Exercise Gym	
27	Upper West Side	Club	

TOKEN #	NEIGHBORHOOD	STOREFRONT	
28	Upper West Side	Bar	
29	Upper West Side	Restaurant	
30	Morningside	Bar	
31	Morningside	Restaurant	
32	Morningside	Exercise Gym	
33	Harlem	Warehouse	
34	Harlem	Restaurant	
35	Manhattan Village	Abandoned Apartment	
36	El Barrio	Bowling Alley	
37	El Barrio	Exercise Gym	

SKYSCRAPER TOKENS

Skyscraper Tokens are virtually ubiquitous throughout the city. There are a total of 150 Skyscraper Tokens resting on the ledges, rooftops, satellite dishes, and antennas of the city's tallest buildings. Some of the larger buildings

have as many as five separate Skyscraper Tokens atop their upper reaches; check all four (or more) sides of each ledge during the ascent to the skyscraper's top.

The map provided shows the distribution of all 150 Skyscraper Tokens, each of which is worth 50 Hero Points if found. Many of the tokens are spaced closely together and may be represented on the map by a single icon. The best way to collect Skyscraper Tokens is to simply keep your eyes peeled and to occasionally spend some time checking out all of the various ledges on the different buildings. Skyscraper Tokens aren't always near the top of the building, and can in fact be found much lower.

BUOY TOKENS

Secret Tokens are the hardest group of Exploration Tokens to find, but Buoy Tokens are definitely the hardest to actually obtain. There are 130 Buoy Tokens hovering atop the myriad of buoys that encircle Manhattan Island (and Roosevelt Island). These buoys are just off the coast of the island, and are only several times the width of Spider-Man in diameter. Spider-Man must make a running leap from solid ground and accurately land on the buoy's base, else he'll splash down in the water. Once on the buoy, leap straight into the air to claim the Buoy Token.

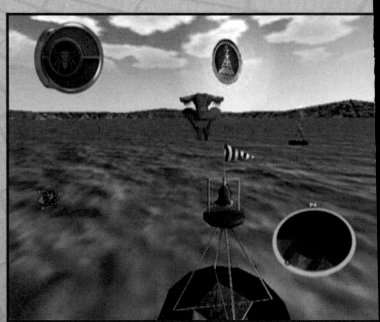

The best way to go about collecting the Buoy Tokens is to face an off-shore buoy and fully charge the Jump Meter. Then hold the Sprint Button and let fly from the edge of the island. Immediately begin holding the Grab Button as Spider-Man flings through the air to keep his momentum from carrying him off the buoy. Be careful when landing on the buoy, as it's easy to make him accidentally crawl down into the water. Touching the water will force Spider-Man back onto the island, necessitating another attempt at the Buoy Token.

The accompanying map shows the distribution of all 130 Buoy Tokens. Several buoys have two Buoy Tokens hovering above them and are represented by a single icon on the map. Some of the buoys can be reached only by leaping first to a sailboat in the harbor, but this situation is easy to identify when it is encountered. Each Buoy Token is worth 50 Hero Points when collected.

Awards

Access the Pause Menu and scroll over to the Status Menu to view the list of Awards that Spider-Man can earn. You earn some of these rewards over the course of completing the main story path, but the majority of them will come only through extended play, well after the story has been completed. The following list shows what each Award is, how it's earned, and the number of Hero Points that are awarded for completing the requirements.

Award Requirements and Bonuses

AWARD	REQUIREMENT	HERO POINTS BONUS
Employee of the Month	All Pizza Deliveries	250
Shutterbug	All Photo Missions	250
Knowledge Seeker	All Hint Markers	250
Silver Medalist	All Challenges Beaten	2000
Gold Medalist	All Challenge Mega Times Beaten	5000
Drenched Explorer	All Buoy Tokens	500
Watchful Explorer	All Secret Tokens	2000
Towering Explorer	All Skyscraper Tokens	500
Vigilant Explorer	All Hideout Tokens	1000
Master Explorer	All Exploration Tokens	2000
Friend to Children	25 Balloons Returned	250
Peace Maker	25 Gang Wars Prevented	250
Bane of Petty Thieves	25 Purse Snatches Prevented	250
Thug Mugger	25 Muggings Prevented	250
Watch Dog	25 Break-Ins Foiled	250
Anger Manager	25 Road Rages Stopped	250
Stick Up Artist	25 Robberies Foiled	250
Partycrasher	25 Battles Royal Stopped	250
Lifter of Spirits	25 Hanging Citizens Rescued	250
Sucker	25 Ambushes Foiled	250
Automobile Avenger	25 Car Jackings Stopped	250
Life Preserver	25 Sinking Boat Crises Resolved	250
Human Ambulance	25 Medical Emergencies Resolved	250
Honorary Deputy	25 Officer Assists Completed	250
Crime Stopper	250 Petty Crimes Stopped	250
Good Samaritan	250 Citizens in Distress Helped	250
Champ	200 Enemies Defeated	250
Mega Champ	500 Enemies Defeated	250
Big Game Hunter	Rhino Defeated	250
Alien Buster	Mysterio Defeated	250
Shock Absorber	Shocker Defeated	250
Tentacle Wrangler	Doc Ock Defeated	250
Speed Freak	Max Swing Speed	250
Hardcore Gamer	All Arcade Games	0
Lover not a Fighter	Complete all the Mary Jane Missions	250
Hero in Training	Accumulated 15,000 Hero Points	250
Hero	Accumulated 45,000 Hero Points	250
Super Hero	Accumulated 100,000 Hero Points	250
Mega Hero	Accumulated 200,000 Hero Points	250
Game Master	Completed Everything in the Game	250

CHAPTER 1:

What Might Have Been

To-Do List

- Learn the Basics.

Mission Objectives

N/A

State of the Story

Welcome back to New York City, the home of Peter Parker and playground of Spider-Man. It's been a while since Spider-Man defeated Green Goblin and much has changed, but not all for the better. Criminals are still determined to take what's not theirs and continue to terrorize the good people of this magnificent city. And while Spider-Man enjoys rounding up these hooligans for the police, his escapades have hampered Peter's relationship with Mary Jane. But enough about that, it's time to rediscover the amazing powers of Spider-Man.

TUTORIAL

MISSION TYPE
Instructional

CHARACTERS INVOLVED
Spider-Man

Spider-Man begins the game on a rooftop in the Lower West Side. Before you can take him swinging through the concrete valleys of the city, you must first learn his most basic maneuvers. After all, one must learn to crawl before one can swing.

Approach the building's wall and press the Grab Button to stick to the wall. Spider-Man can use this technique to crawl along any surface. Once he has begun crawling on the wall, release the Grab Button and use the Movement controls to make him crawl in any direction on the wall. To detach from the wall, either press the Jump Button or simply crawl back down to the street or up to a ledge or rooftop above.

The next skill to learn is jumping. Move onto a flat surface and press the Jump Button. Tapping the Jump Button will make Spider-Man hop several feet off the ground, but that's not all he can do. Try holding the Jump Button to charge the Jump Meter (yellow bar). The longer the button is held, the higher Spider-Man will leap into the air when the button is released. Practice releasing the button at different times to get a feel for the various heights he can attain.

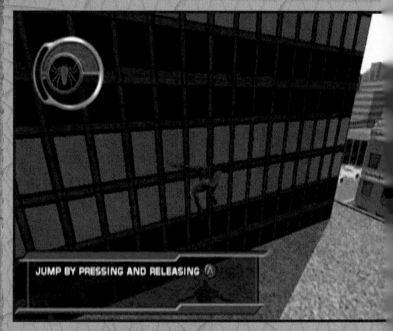

JUMP BY PRESSING AND RELEASING Ⓐ

JUMP BY PRESSING AND RELEASING Ⓐ

Now that you know how to make Spider-Man crawl and jump, it's time to approach the first Destination Marker. Look at the Mini Map and note the length of the lines connected to the blue dot and the red dot. Because the blue dot's line is much longer (i.e. higher) it tells you that Spider-Man is below the Destination Marker.

Begin crawling up the wall, and hold the Jump Button to fully charge the Jump Meter. Release the Jump Button to make Spider-Man leap up the side of the building.

WALL CRAWLING 101

If Spider-Man lands on the same wall surface from which he jumped, he will automatically cling and continue crawling up the wall. However, if he jumps from one wall surface to another, you'll have to press the Grab Button when he lands to latch onto the new wall.

Continue climbing up the side of the building and approach the Destination Marker to complete this part of the tutorial.

CHAPTER WRAP-UP

THINGS ARE JUST GETTING STARTED BUT IN CASE YOU FORGOT, THIS CHAPTER WAS ALL ABOUT LEARNING HOW TO CRAWL ON WALLS AND HOW TO JUMP. YOU ALSO LEARNED ABOUT REACHING THE DESTINATION MARKER. THERE'S A LOT MORE TO LEARN ABOUT SPIDER-MAN, SO HURRY UP AND TURN THE PAGE!

CHAPTER 8:

A Day in the Life

To-Do List

- Fight Crime.
- Buy Swing Speed Upgrade from Store.

Mission Objectives

N/A

State of the Story

Not much has happened in the past few minutes, but Spider-Man's Spider Senses tell him that trouble is brewing not too far in the future.

TUTORIAL CONTINUED

MISSION TYPE
Instructional

CHARACTERS INVOLVED
Spider-Man
Street Thugs

Now it's time to learn how to Web Swing. Leap off the building's roof where the large green arrow is. Press the Swing Button when you're instructed to. This will make Spider-Man shoot a webline toward the building across the street. Now he can swing back and forth high above the ground.

Web Swinging is Spider-Man's primary means of travel and is something that you'll grow accustomed to over time. For now, practice swinging back and forth between the nearby buildings. Practice releasing the webline by hitting the Jump Button at different points during the swing to get a feel for how it will affect Spider-Man's momentum.

YOU CAN CHARGE YOUR JUMP WHILE SWINGING BY HOLDING

EASY SWINGING

If you have Easy Swinging turned on in the Options menu, Spider-Man will automatically jump from his webline when you release the Swing Button.

Ideally, you should charge the Jump Meter and release the Jump Button just before Spider-Man reaches the furthest point in his swing. This way, he'll be catapulted forward through the air. Press the Swing Button while he's airborne to make Spider-Man shoot another webline to continue swinging down the street. Use the movement controls to precisely control Spider-Man while he's swinging, and to help increase his momentum. Try swinging around the block and through some of the narrow alleys.

Before long, Spider-Man will be alerted to a robbery in progress near the arcade. The crooks are trying to flee in their vehicle and it's up to Spider-Man to stop them! Chase after the blue Destination Marker by Web Swinging after them. Hold the Sprint Button for a swing boost, and charge the Jump Meter to get as much momentum between swings as possible.

Once Spider-Man catches up to the getaway car, the four thieves try to escape on foot. Use the Attack Button to knock them out with a series of punches and kicks. Press the Web Button to Web-Trap one so that Spider-Man can beat another into submission.

After three of the four are defeated, Spider-Man is instructed to sprint after the one remaining thug and press the Attack Button while springing (Spring Button + any direction on the Left Analog Stick). This unleashes a tremendous uppercut that sends the thug soaring into the air. Leap into the air after him and press the Attack Button several times to knock him out.

Spider-Man reclaims the stolen money when the fourth thug is incapacitated. Return the money to the arcade owner by heading to the Destination Marker that has appeared. The owner thanks Spider-Man and invites him to his arcade to play games any time he wishes—on the house of course!

USING THE MAP

Follow the on-screen instructions and inspect the Zoom Map. This map contains a wealth of information and should be viewed often. For now, note the location of the Upgrade Store (marked by a large "S" on the map) in the Lower West Side. This is Spider-Man's next target.

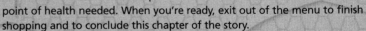

Exit the map and follow the blue Destination Marker to the Upgrade Store. It's only a couple of blocks away, to the northeast. The Upgrade Store is actually a comic book shop and, fortunately, it's still in business. Go through the doors, approach the icon on the left, and press the Attack Button to access the store's list of Hero Upgrades.

Select the Swing Speed Level 1 upgrade and purchase it for 50 Hero Points. The Full Health healing upgrade will also be available if Spider-Man currently doesn't have all 200 of his health points. The health upgrade heals Spider-Man at a cost of 1 Hero Point per point of health needed. When you're ready, exit out of the menu to finish shopping and to conclude this chapter of the story.

CHAPTER WRAP-UP

NOW YOU ARE TRULY GETTING A FEEL FOR CONTROLLING SPIDER-MAN! THIS CHAPTER SHOWED YOU HOW TO MAKE SPIDER-MAN SWING FROM A WEBLINE AND IT ALSO CONTAINED THE FIRST OF MANY BATTLES AGAINST THE CITY'S RUFFIANS. BEST OF ALL, SPIDER-MAN GOT TO VISIT THE UPGRADE STORE FOR THE FIRST TIME. CONTROLLING HIM WITH THE SWING SPEED LEVEL 1 UPGRADE WILL REQUIRE SOME FASTER REFLEXES, BUT IT'S NOTHING YOU CAN'T HANDLE. THIS CONCLUDES THE TUTORIAL PORTION, SO PREPARE TO TAKE FULL CONTROL OF SPIDER-MAN; NEW YORK CITY IS DEPENDING ON YOU!

CHAPTER 3:

Punctuality is the Thief of Time

To-Do List

- Go to Pizza Parlor.
- Earn 2000 More Hero Points.

Mission Objectives

Late for Class
Peter's Birthday
Hello Black Cat

State of the Story

Being a college student, a pizza delivery boy, and a superhero (not to mention a photographer) is hard work and can often strain one's relationships. This is the predicament that Peter Parker now faces. His desire to use his powers for good is at odds with leading the normal life of a college student. On the one hand, there is plenty of time for him to accomplish everything he *NEEDS* to do in a day, but on the other, the things he *WANTS* to do often get neglected. Even superheroes can't be everywhere at once.

LATE FOR CLASS

MISSION TYPE:
Swing-To, Beat 'Em Up, and Swing-To

CHARACTERS INVOLVED:
Spider-Man
Female Civilian
Street Thugs
Peter Parker
Dr. Connors

Soon after this chapter begins, Spider-Man remembers that Peter is late for his class with Dr. Connors. The Blue Destination marker indicates that Spider-Man must head north from the Lower West Side up toward the Morningside neighborhood, where the university is. It's a long haul, so get going! Swing above the center of the main avenue. Fully charge the Jump Meter as you swing to make the most of Spider-Man's momentum.

PULL **R** TO SWING, THEN **A** NEAR THE TOP OF YOUR SWING. FLY THROUGH THE AIR, THEN START SWINGING AGAIN WITH **R**

Just as Spider-Man reaches Morningside, a cry for help calls out from the east and the Destination Marker suddenly shifts locations. Hurry in this new direction to answer the call.

A second wave of enemies soon appears, and they waste no time in ganging up on Spider-Man. Activate Spider Reflexes and look for the red circle to indicate an incoming attack. Quickly press the Grab Button to dodge the attack, and retaliate with a Counter Flip Kick by tapping the Attack Button during the dodge. A well-timed Counter Uppercut may even knock multiple enemies into the air simultaneously; this will really tilt the battle in Spider-Man's favor!

Spider-Man arrives just in time to witness several thugs chasing after a young lady with an important-looking briefcase. Perform the Sprint Uppercut on the nearest hoodlum, and then knock him out with a series of body blows while he's airborne. Press the Sprint Button and Web Button to blast another enemy with the Web Trap, and then take care of the remaining thugs in this wave.

An eighth and final thug tries to flee down the street with the lady's briefcase. Chase after him and beat him into submission with a Sprint Uppercut and a barrage of punches. Return the case to the lady.

The original Destination Marker reappears once Spider-Man has thwarted the muggers. Follow the marker to the university and locate the Change Icon on the rooftop to strip off the costume so Peter Parker can meet with Dr. Connors.

ULL ® TO SWING, THEN Ⓐ NEAR THE TOP F YOUR SWING. FLY THROUGH THE AIR, THEN TART SWINGING AGAIN WITH ®

SPIDER-MAN'S FREE TIME

Spider-Man isn't always rushing off to stop would-be thieves or attend important meetings on time. In fact, much of Spider-Man's time is his own to do with it as he wishes. It is during this time, between missions, where you must exercise his great powers (and great responsibility) to increase his stash of Hero Points. This is the time when Spider-Man should concentrate on the tasks outlined in the To-Do List.

Because one of the items on the To-Do List requires a visit to the pizza parlor, a white Destination Marker appears on the Mini Map. Slowly proceed downtown toward the pizza parlor near the waterfront on the Lower West Side. On the way there, participate in several Voluntary Missions and activate as many Hint Markers as possible to earn the requisite Hero Points. Voluntary Missions often reward as many as 250 Hero Points, while the ubiquitous Hint Markers yield 10 Hero Points and some valuable advice.

VOLUNTARY MISSIONS

Many upstanding New York citizens have green question marks hovering above their heads. Stopping to speak with them will trigger a Voluntary Mission. There are many types of Voluntary Missions ranging from assisting the police in a shootout to bringing someone to the hospital. Spider-Man earns significant Hero Points by completing these tasks so don't overlook them. Voluntary Missions are covered in greater detail in this guide's Superhero Training chapter.

Try to rack up over 1600 Hero Points en route to the pizza parlor. Go to the side of the restaurant facing the water and use the Change Icon to turn back to Peter Parker. This triggers the start of Pizza Mission 1. Peter's first delivery is very straightforward and should not pose any difficulty. Head toward the yellow Destination Marker that appears on the map, and take care not to fall from great heights. Use the Wall Slide technique to get safely down to the ground after a Web Swing.

PIZZA MISSIONS

Peter Parker isn't just a college student; he's also a pizza delivery boy and a freelance photographer! Pizza Missions require Peter (as Spider-Man) to deliver a certain number of pizzas to specific addresses in the city. The delivery must be made and the bag must be returned empty within a set amount of time. Furthermore, care must be taken not to jostle

the pizzas while they are strapped to Spider-Man's back. Each Pizza Mission is covered in this guide's The Hero's Work is Never Done chapter.

Head toward the Theatre District after successfully delivering the pizza. Continue earning additional Hero Points by completing Voluntary Missions. It's also wise to keep your eyes and ears peeled for the purple Destination Markers that tip off the location of a Petty Crime. Petty Crimes are similar to Voluntary Missions, but are usually smaller in scale and threat.

Once you're in the Theatre District, follow the main roads to where they intersect up ahead. This is the most brightly lit area of the city and should be recognizable to those who have been there. Look for the enormous Activision and Treyarch signs and the fork in the large road. Locate the Challenge Icon on the sidewalk where the roads diverge. This particular Challenge (Race #91) is perfect for beginners and nets Spider-Man another 300 Hero Points for regular time and 500 points for mega time.

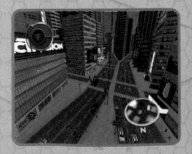

CHALLENGE RACES

There are over a hundred different Challenges throughout the city, each offering Spider-Man a unique obstacle course and time limit. They each have different difficulty ratings, and players are advised to stick with Challenges rated "Easy" in the early going until they acquire additional locomotion upgrades. Challenge Races can be restarted at any time. See the The Hero's Work is Never Done chapter in this guide for a detailed breakdown of every Challenge.

PETER'S BIRTHDAY

MISSION TYPE
Swing-To

CHARACTERS INVOLVED
Spider-Man
Peter Parker
Mary Jane
Harry Osborn

As night falls across the city, and Spider-Man's Hero Points crest the 1,000 mark, he suddenly remembers that he is supposed to meet Mary Jane and Harry tonight to celebrate Peter's Birthday. Quickly head toward the Garment District and Midtown to the blue Destination Marker.

THE YELLOW BAR NEXT TO THE HEALTH METER SHOWS THE POWER OF THE CHARGED JUMP.

Locate the Change Icon on the building's roof to strip out of the Spider-Man costume. Peter lets himself off the rooftop and rushes over to meet Mary Jane and Harry. The three catch up on each other's lives and then head inside to celebrate Peter's birthday over dinner.

SPIDER-MAN'S FREE TIME

Dinner is over and the night is still young. Check the To-Do List to see how many Hero Points you need to reach this chapter's requirement. Then drop down to street level to see if anyone needs assistance.

THE AGONY OF DEFEAT

Beware that Spider-Man loses 100 Hero Points if he fails a Voluntary Mission.

HELLO BLACK CAT

MISSION TYPE
Swing-To, Beat 'Em Up, and Chase

CHARACTERS INVOLVED
Spider-Man
Art Thieves
Black Cat

Shortly after the To-Do List is completed, Spider-Man remembers that he promised to meet Mary Jane to get tickets for her show. Swing in the direction of the blue Destination Marker, toward the Chelsea neighborhood. This leads Spider-Man to a Change Icon in a secluded alley. It's time to become Peter Parker again.

During his meeting with Mary Jane, Peter notices a band of crooks suspiciously sneaking into a nearby art gallery. Much to Mary Jane's dismay, Peter suddenly runs off—something she's getting a little too familiar with him doing.

Run across the street toward the Destination Marker and enter the art gallery to confront the art thieves. You must deal with eight thugs, but some of them have guns, so approach them with caution. Fortunately, the gallery has two floors so Spider-Man can take care of those on the ground level first, leaving those with guns on the upper level for later.

Enter the gallery and proceed to the left to deal with the three thugs on that side of the room. Use the Web Yank maneuver to disarm them of their melee weapons, and then proceed to beat them into submission. Leap onto the balcony above to thwart the two art thieves up there. One of them has a gun so be ready to either Web Yank the gun from his hands or switch to Spider Reflexes to get an edge in dodging the bullets.

Return to the far side of the gallery's main floor to deal with the final three crooks. Each of them has a gun so be ready to utilize those Spider Reflexes. Actively tap the Dodge Button to dodge each of the bullets as they whiz past Spider-Man's head. Relieve them of their guns and then finish them off with some superhero punches and kicks!

Once Spider-Man has firmly dealt with the thugs, he meets a saucy feline by the name of Black Cat. He follows her to the rooftop where a chase ensues. Black Cat can run and leap as skillfully as Spider-Man can, if not better, and it's up to you to make sure he keeps up with her. Follow Black Cat from rooftop to rooftop to try and figure out who, or what, she is.

The large meter that appears on the top right-hand corner of the screen indicates Spider-Man's proximity to Black Cat. Although he can't actually catch her before she decides to stop, he can fall too far behind and fail the mission. Fortunately for Spider-Man, she leaves a glowing white trail that betrays her position. Follow this glittering streak from building to building to keep up with her. Spider-Man needs to use all of his jumping and web-slinging skills to successfully clear each of the jumps that Black Cat makes.

THE CHASE BEGINS

The only way to keep up with Black Cat is to exploit Spider-Man's jumping ability. Fully charge nearly every jump. Use Web Swinging carefully to stay on Black Cat's trail. If you're coming up short on a jump, press toward the building's side and hold the Sprint and Grab buttons to make Spider-Man begin sprinting up the wall. Charge the Jump Meter while Wall Running to leap up to the rooftop! If all else fails, press the Grab Button to crawl on the wall, but this is much slower than Wall Running.

RUNNING ROOM

There will be times when Spider-Man needs a fully-charged running jump, but the roof's edge is too close to allow for much of a runway. Stand still and hold the Jump Button to charge the jump, then sprint toward the edge and quickly release the Jump Button to get as much momentum as possible.

Black Cat eventually stops (after roughly two dozen leaps) if Spider-Man manages to keep up with her. She then proceeds to tease Spider-Man right to his face. Regardless of how *standard* she feels Spider-Man is, he succeeded in keeping up with this wily masked cat. They'll meet again, that much is certain.

CHAPTER WRAP-UP

WHAT A WAY TO SPEND ONE'S BIRTHDAY! SURE, DINNER WAS GREAT, BUT PETER PARKER FOUND OUT THAT MARY JANE, THE LOVE OF HIS LIFE, IS NOW SEEING ANOTHER MAN. AND THEN, TO CONFUSE MATTERS, SPIDER-MAN MEETS A SEDUCTIVE WOMAN NAMED BLACK CAT WHO APPEARS TO HAVE SUPER POWERS ON PAR WITH HIS OWN. COULD IT BE? DESPITE HIS TROUBLED LOVE LIFE, SPIDER-MAN CAN TAKE SOLACE IN KNOWING THAT HE HAS CLOSE TO 3000 HERO POINTS TO SPEND IN THE NEXT CHAPTER! HE ALSO HAS THE SENSE OF ACCOMPLISHMENT THAT COMES FROM HELPING A LOT OF PEOPLE AND SUCCESSFULLY DELIVERING HIS FIRST PIZZA. MAMMA MIA, WHAT A DAY!

CHAPTER 4:

All in a Day's Work

To-Do List

- Talk to Jameson at the Daily Bugle.
- Buy Level 2 Swing Speed Upgrade from Store.
- Earn 3000 More Hero Points.

Mission Objectives

Hello Jameson
Rhino Rampage

State of the Story

Although Peter would like to spend his day tracking down that mysterious Black Cat he met, he really must try to get some additional work from the Daily Bugle. With a little luck, he might be able to make some extra money with his camera.

HELLO JAMESON

MISSION TYPE
Swing-To, Photo Mission

CHARACTERS INVOLVED
Spider-Man
Peter Parker
Mr. Jameson
Robbie Robertson

It's been a while since Peter Parker last spoke with Mr. Jameson at the Daily Bugle and although Peter doesn't have any photos to sell, there is a chance that Peter can get an assignment from him. Spider-Man begins this chapter just two blocks from the Daily Bugle, but equally important is the fact that an Upgrade Store is just a couple of blocks further south, in the Flat Iron district (see map).

Spider-Man didn't make any purchases in the previous chapter, so head to the Upgrade Store and buy up every Combat and Locomotion Upgrade it has in stock—there are more than enough Hero Points to cover this shopping spree. At the very least, purchase the Swing Speed Level 2 upgrade to complete the task on the To-Do List.

SHOPPING FOR SPIDER-MAN

The following Hero Upgrades can all be purchased at this point in the game: Swing Speed Level 2, Web Zip, Slingshot Jump, Inverted Widow (air trick), Super Fly Spider Guy (air trick), Grapple, Air Jump Off Kick, Cannonball Kick, and Multi-Web Tie Level 1. Depending on how many Voluntary Missions you completed, there should still be roughly 2,000 Hero Points remaining after making all of these purchases.

Once you're done shopping, return to the Daily Bugle by following the white Destination Marker on the screen. Climb to the rooftop and approach the central ventilation unit to uncover a secret Spider-Man entrance. Drop down into the ductwork to enter the men's restroom where Spider-Man will automatically change back to Peter Parker.

TIME TO VOLUNTEER

Although it's not necessary to do so, Spider-Man can benefit from completing a Voluntary Mission or two before entering the Daily Bugle. Not only will it help him earn the 3000 Hero Points specified on the To-Do List, but it's also a great time to put some of those new Combat Upgrades to use.

Exit the bathroom and head down the hall on the left to the Daily Bugle's newsroom. Talk to Mr. Jameson's assistant at the desk on the left to get permission to meet with him. Despite claims to the contrary, Mr. Jameson is his typical gruff self and is in no mood to meet with Peter. Fortunately for Peter, a friendly editor named Robbie has an assignment for him. Robbie wants a series of photos taken from atop the tallest building in the city. Exit the newsroom and use the Change Icon in the restroom to turn back to Spider-Man.

The specified skyscraper is located just three blocks north of the Daily Bugle. Follow the yellow Destination Marker to the first Camera Icon located approximately one-third of the way up the building's side. Crawl along the face of the building to the marker and press the Attack Button to take the photograph.

Head clockwise around the building and continue climbing to reach the second Camera Icon. The third icon is still higher and on a ledge in the building's northwest corner. There are two more Camera Icons left to hit: one at the base of the antenna tower, and another on top of the antenna. Welcome to the top of New York City!

SKYSCRAPER TOKENS

The first of 150 Skyscraper Tokens is located atop this building's antenna. The majority of the Skyscraper Tokens are located in Midtown, in and around New York City's tallest skyscrapers. Keep an eye out for them whenever Spider-Man is atop one of the taller buildings in the city. Be sure to check out this guide's The Hero's Work is Never Done chapter and the map on the accompanying poster for all 150 locations!

Once you've taken the fifth and final photograph, carefully dive off the top of the antenna into the concrete valleys below. Swing south back to the Daily Bugle and drop through the rooftop ventilation system to stealthily reenter the building. Return to the newsroom to show the photos to Robbie. Once Peter has Robbie's approval, cross the room to Mr. Jameson's office and talk to his assistant. She'll send Peter in to show the photos to Mr. Jameson.

Mr. Jameson will eventually accept the photos and Peter will be free to leave. Return to the restroom to change back into Spider-Man.

RHINO RAMPAGE

MISSION TYPE
Boss Battle

CHARACTERS INVOLVED
Spider-Man, Rhino

Spider-Man exits the Daily Bugle just in time to witness a huge plume of smoke from a distant explosion. He rushes to the scene of the commotion and finds an oversized brawler by the name of Rhino.

Rhino Rampage

BOSS BATTLE: RHINO

BOSS ATTACK	DAMAGE TO SPIDER-MAN
Metal Column Swing	Moderate
Charging Horn Attack	High
Thrown Metal Column	Low

Rhino is considerably larger than Spider-Man and he boasts some very thick armor as well. If that isn't bad enough, he totes an enormous metal column that he uses as a bat. Fortunately for Spider-Man, Rhino isn't nearly as sharp as the horn he sports on his costume!

The key to success lies in identifying Rhino's three basic attacks. Rhino's primary attack, and the one he begins the battle with, consists of him spinning around in a circle three times while swinging the giant metal column at Spider-Man. Stand roughly two steps away, wait for him to begin swinging, and then press the Grab Button when Spider-Man's head flashes. Dodge each of the three swings, and then attack with a flurry of punches and kicks while Rhino is dizzy.

A FLASHING HEAD MEANS DODGE!

Spider-Man's head flash signals that his Spider Senses foresee an incoming attack. Press the Grab Button in a timely manner to dodge an imminent assault. This opens up an opportunity to counterattack Spider-Man's foe.

Rhino's second most common attack is his charge. He'll hunker down and raise his horn a few times before initiating his stampede. Charge the Jump Meter ever so slightly and leap over him as he rushes Spider-Man. Spider-Man's head will flash and, if performed correctly, a quick tap of the Grab Button will make Spider-Man deliver a swift kick to Rhino's head as he passes below. Best of all, dodging the charge will often leave Rhino confused and vulnerable to a follow-up attack.

MID-FLIGHT RECOVERY

No matter how hard you try to keep Spider-Man safe from Rhino's attacks, he's likely to connect with one of them and send Spider-Man flying through the air like a ragdoll. Repeatedly tap the Grab Button to make Spider-Man recover before he hits the ground and loses more health.

Rhino's remaining attack is somewhat harder to predict, but can be avoided nonetheless. He reaches back and throws the metal column in a boomerang fashion. Charge the Jump Meter and leap high into the air over the incoming projectile. Look for Spider-Man's head to flash and press the Grab Button to perform a quick evasive maneuver. With some luck, the metal column will come back and hit Rhino, thereby dazing him yet again. Drop back to the ground and finish him off once and for all.

WHEN SPIDEYS HEAD FLASHES, PRESS THE ⑧ BUTTON

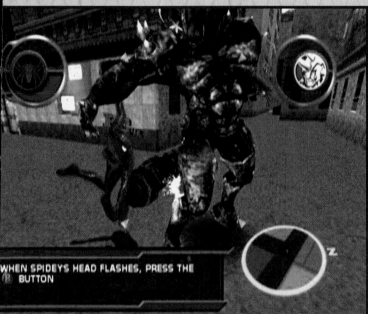

WHEN SPIDEYS HEAD FLASHES, PRESS THE ⑧ BUTTON

BIG GAME HUNTER AWARD

Defeating Rhino will earn Spider-Man the Big Game Hunter award. Check the Awards Screen in the Start Menu to see a list of all of the dozens of awards that can be earned.

SPIDER-MAN'S FREE TIME

Spider-Man is likely in need of some healing. So, head back to the Upgrade Store near the Daily Bugle and purchase Full Health to heal the damage that Rhino inflicted.

Check the To-Do List to see how many more Hero Points you need to complete the last task on the list, and then set out to complete Voluntary Missions to meet your quota. Thanks to the 1,500 Hero Points awarded for defeating Rhino, it shouldn't take long at all!

CHAPTER WRAP-UP

THANKS TO SPIDER-MAN'S AMAZING WALL CRAWLING ABILITIES, PETER PARKER WAS ABLE TO IMPRESS ROBBIE AT THE DAILY BUGLE WITH SOME INCREDIBLE SHOTS FROM ATOP THE TALLEST POINT IN THE CITY. PETER CAN VISIT ROBBIE FOR PHOTO ASSIGNMENTS IN THE FUTURE. ROBBIE WON'T ALWAYS HAVE AN ASSIGNMENT FOR PETER, BUT IT DOESN'T HURT TO SWING BY EVERY NOW AND THEN TO FIND OUT.

CHAPTER 5:

A Meeting of the Minds

To-Do List

- Go to Doctor Octavius's Apartment.
- Buy Grapple Attack Upgrade from Store.
- Earn 2000 More Hero Points.

Mission Objectives

Meet Octavius

State of the Story

Thanks to Harry's connections, Peter has a meeting with Dr. Octavius planned today! Dr. Octavius is working on a phenomenal energy project and Peter can't wait to travel uptown to his apartment to see it.

MEET OCTAVIUS

MISSION TYPE
Swing-To

CHARACTERS INVOLVED
Spider-Man
Peter Parker
Harry Osborn
Otto Octavius
Rosie Octavius

The rumble with Rhino was an unexpected diversion, but fortunately it didn't cut into Peter's plans to have Harry introduce him to Dr. Octavius. Head north from the Daily Bugle, following the white Destination Marker.

PRE-PURCHASED GRAPPLE

We suggested purchasing the Grapple upgrade during the store visit in the previous chapter. If you followed our advice, the item on the To-Do List is already checked off so you have nothing to worry about. If you still need to acquire this valuable upgrade, visit the same Department Store just north of the Daily Bugle (where this chapter begins) and spend some Hero Points to meet the requirement.

PRACTICE THE WEB ZIP

The trip uptown to Dr. Octavius's apartment is a long one. Enjoy the scenery along the way and practice the Web Zip technique to get familiar with one of Spider-Man's most useful abilities. Consider crossing through the heart of Central Park. Stop at each of the Hint Markers located there to gain some additional information and to rack up some

additional Hero Points. Try to Web Zip from treetop to treetop—swing off the first tree, press and hold the Sprint Button, and intermittently tap the Swing Button. This makes Spider-Man shoot a web to the treetop in front of him and yank himself forward. This is a great way to quickly cross the park—just watch out for the lake!

Dr. Octavius's apartment is an enormous building on the Upper West Side, directly across the park from the large museum. Locate the Change Icon on the northeast corner of his building's roof.

Thanks to Harry, Peter gets to meet Dr. Otto Octavius and his wife Rosie. Dr. Octavius shows Peter his perpetual energy invention, but is unfortunately terribly busy and doesn't have time to fully explain what the machine's "arms" do. Perhaps another time…

SPIDER-MAN'S FREE TIME

The meeting with Dr. Octavius didn't last as long as Peter had hoped and now he finds himself uptown with some time to kill. This is a great opportunity to sightsee on the city's north side and to complete some Voluntary Missions. Consider performing a clockwise lap around Central Park's outskirts to get a feel for the Manhattan Village and El Barrio neighborhoods while earning more Hero Points.

Once Spider-Man has at least 1,000 of the 2,000 required Hero Points for this chapter, head back to the Lower West Side and visit Mr. Aziz at the pizza parlor. Complete several Pizza Missions to earn some additional Hero Points and to gain some more practice using Spider-Man's special locomotion maneuvers. Just remember to not jostle those pizzas!

OH BUOY!

Believe it or not, there are still a number of ways to earn Hero Points that we haven't even discussed yet! Notice the shiny objects on all of the buoys in the water by the pizza parlor? Those are Buoy Tokens and each one earns Spider-Man an extra 50 Hero Points. There are 130 Buoy Tokens spread around the perimeter of Manhattan Island, and it's up to you to collect them all! See this guide's The Hero's Work is Never Done chapter for more information concerning Buoy Tokens.

CHAPTER WRAP-UP

PETER PARKER'S MEETING WITH DR. OCTAVIUS REALLY EXCITED PETER, BUT IT WAS TOO BAD DR. CONNORS HAD TO TELL OTTO ABOUT PETER FALLING ASLEEP IN CLASS—HOW EMBARRASSING! WHY DID HARRY CUT THE MEETING SHORT LIKE THAT? DID HE KNOW PETER HAD PIZZAS TO DELIVER? NEVERTHELESS, IT WASN'T A WASTED DAY BY ANY MEANS; SPIDER-MAN ACQUIRED SOME MORE HERO POINTS AND HE GOT TO EXPLORE PARTS OF THE CITY HE HADN'T VISITED YET.

CHAPTER 8:

Cat and Mouse

To-Do List

- Find the 5 Photo Op Tokens.
- Go to Mary Jane's Apartment.
- Buy Level 3 Swing Speed Upgrade from Store.
- Earn 2000 More Hero Points.

Mission Objectives

Beginner Photo Op
Black Cat Jewelry
Movies with Mary Jane

State of the Story

It won't be easy, but maybe Peter can balance his life behind the mask with his social life. Mary Jane won't give him too many more chances before she closes the door on him for good, so he'd better not be late for their date today. Hopefully, the menaces of the city will cooperate and put their evil deeds on hold for a little while.

BEGINNER PHOTO OP

MISSION TYPE
Photo Hunt

CHARACTERS INVOLVED
Spider-Man

This chapter begins with two Destination Markers visible on the screen: the white one directs Spider-Man to Mary Jane's apartment while the yellow one depicts five Photo Op Tokens. Ignore the white Destination Marker for now and swing across the city toward the yellow one at Greenwich Village.

As Spider-Man draws closer to the Photo Op Tokens, the singular yellow Destination Marker splits into five. Swing and Web Zip from roof to roof to collect them all to complete this task. Each token is located on one of the buildings near the large grassy quad in the village. When you've collected the fifth one, a message appears to alert you that all of the Beginner Camera Tokens have been found.

BLACK CAT JEWELRY

MISSION TYPE
Chase

CHARACTERS INVOLVED
Spider-Man

Black Cat

Just as Spider-Man concludes his impromptu photo safari, an alarm rings out from the Uptown Jewelry store. Lo and behold, none other than Black Cat is seen leaving the premises! It's time to kick it into overdrive; she's getting away!

Black Cat enjoys playing hard to get and, as Spider-Man is about to find out, she's quite good at it. This chase is much more difficult for Spider-Man, as the route she takes is trickier than the first. Spider-Man must react to Black Cat's many redirections quickly if he hopes to keep her in sight. Furthermore, he'll have to use his Web Zip technique to reach some of the more distant rooftops.

Follow Black Cat across the night sky, past the Daily Bugle and ultimately to a rooftop just north of the large skyscraper in the Theatre District.

DON'T LET GREED DISTRACT YOU

It's possible to collect several Skyscraper Tokens during the chase by sticking closely to Black Cat's chosen path, but don't risk losing her over it. The tokens will always be there later.

MOVIES WITH MARY JANE

MISSION TYPE
Swing-To

CHARACTERS INVOLVED
Spider-Man
Peter Parker
Mary Jane

Spider-Man has to get those thoughts of Black Cat out of his head because he's got a date with Mary Jane. In fact, he's actually starting to run a little late. Note the white Destination Marker on the screen and start Web Swinging south toward Soho where Mary Jane's apartment is.

A QUICK DETOUR

Pay a quick visit to the Department Store in the Garment District to purchase the Hero Upgrades that have opened up since Chapter 4's conclusion. Spider-Man should have more than enough Hero Points to purchase each of the following: Rising Knee Kick, Yank Behind, Earth Breaker Punch, Level 3 Air Combo, and Launch Kick.

THE QUICK WAY TO THE TOP

It's much faster to use the Web Zip to catapult onto a rooftop (or close to it) than it is to swing into the side of a building and crawl up.

Run up to the front door of Mary Jane's apartment building to find the note she left for Peter. She didn't know whether Peter planned to meet her at her apartment or at the theatre so she went ahead without him. The movie starts in 40 seconds—get moving!

The movie theatre is only a few blocks away, but Spider-Man had better move if he wants to make it in time. Hold the Sprint Button and jump into the air. Use the Web Zip technique to stay airborne and avoid traffic. Glance at the Mini Map to determine the most direct path, and use a few Web Swings to round the last corner toward the theatre. Access the Change Icon behind the theatre to take off the costume. Peter will run around to the front of the theatre in time to surprise Mary Jane with his punctuality.

SPIDER-MAN'S FREE TIME

Between the Hero Points awarded for successfully keeping up with Black Cat and for completing the other missions in this chapter, Spider-Man shouldn't need too many more to reach the requirement. Look for Voluntary Missions near the theatre, and keep an eye out for purple Destination Markers that signal the occurrence of a Petty Crime. Petty Crimes are usually easier to resolve and are a good source of quick Hero Points.

CHAPTER WRAP-UP

ROBBIE AND MR. JAMESON AREN'T THE ONLY ONES WHO CAN MAKE PETER AND SPIDER-MAN TAKE PHOTOS. EVERY ONCE IN A WHILE, SPIDER-MAN TAKES SOME PHOTOS ON HIS OWN ACCORD TO STAY SHARP—PLUS, IT PAYS TO HAVE SOME EXTRAS READY FOR JAMESON. BUT JAMESON IS NOT WHO IS ON PETER'S MIND RIGHT NOW; THAT WOULD BE MARY JANE AND BLACK CAT. HOW'S A SUPERHERO TO CHOOSE BETWEEN THE GIRL NEXT DOOR AND A LADY AS MYSTERIOUS AS HIMSELF?

B Train

CHAPTER 7:

Pride and Prejudice

To-Do List

- Talk to Jameson at the Daily Bugle.
- Earn 3000 More Hero Points.

Mission Objectives

Quentin Beck Biathlon

State of the Story

The problem with being a superhero is that everyone is always gunning for you. Sure, there are the happy citizens glad to have a superhero around when they're dangling from scaffolding or when their kid's balloon flies away, but a lot of people are far too jealous for their own good. Quentin Beck is one such person...

QUENTIN BECK BIATHLON

MISSION TYPE
Swing-To, Contest

CHARACTERS INVOLVED
Spider-Man
Peter Parker
Mr. Jameson
Quentin Beck

Mr. Jameson needs to meet with Peter right away, so swing across town to the Daily Bugle as soon as the chapter begins. Follow the white Destination Marker back to the Daily Bugle's roof to enter the building and talk with Mr. Jameson in the newsroom.

Quentin Beck has arranged quite a spectacle to showcase his latest gadgetry and disprove Spider-Man's "super powers." He has planned a contest featuring two very different events. The first contest tests Spider-Man's ability to round up criminals and deposit them in color-coded holding chambers. The second contest is an elaborate obstacle course.

SPOILER WARNING!

Do you have the feeling that something seems just a little *off* with this whole biathlon? Well, if so, your Spider Senses are working quite well. Everything about this event is an illusion created by the diabolical Mysterio. And you just thought the people in the bleachers looked like cardboard—they *are* cardboard!

Peter has been hoping for an assignment, and he just got one: get to the sports arena and photograph Spider-Man competing against Quentin Beck! The special effects guru from Hollywood has challenged Spider-Man in hopes of revealing him to the public as a fraud. Return to the restroom, access the Change Icon, and exit to the rooftop. The sports arena is only a few blocks away; locate the blue Destination Marker on the screen and follow it to the arena. Enter the front doors and cross the lobby to the contest area.

CONVICT CORRAL

The "convict round-up" portion of the contest consists of three rounds. Spider-Man and Quentin Beck race to see who can capture the most convicts. The convicts are released from each of the arena's corners and must be thrown into one of the three pits, as indicated by a green glow. Each round features roughly a dozen convicts. Whoever has captured the most at the conclusion of the third round will be crowned the winner. If Spider-Man wins, he advances to the second challenge. If Quentin Beck wins, Spider-Man has to retry this portion of the contest.

HOLD (Y) AND (B) TO REEL ENEMIES INTO YOUR GRASP

HOLD (Y), THEN MOVE THE LEFT THUMBSTICK IN ANY DIRECTION.

The only combat during the contest is between Spider-Man and the convicts; he cannot attack Quentin Beck to make him drop his quarry. To capture a convict, face one in relatively close proximity, and then press the Web and Grab buttons to reel a convict into Spider-Man's arms. Quickly approach the green-glowing pit and press the Grab Button to toss him in, thereby scoring a point. Spider-Man can also use Web Rodeo to fling the convicts into the pits. Make sure that the convict drops into the pit while it is still green, else the point won't count!

Quentin Beck flies around the arena, using his mechanical contraption to round up multiple enemies simultaneously. Occasionally, he even tries to capture one of the enemies that Spider-Man is trying to reel in. When this happens, just let Quentin have him and move on to the next convict—don't bother wasting time trying to play tug of war!

Spider-Man's best chance for success is to rush to meet the convicts as they emerge from one of the corners; the energy barriers flash orange to signal convict releases. Capture one, sprint toward the green pit, and throw in the convict. Then remain near the pit and simply turn, reel in a convict, and drop him into the pit. Repeat this process as many times as possible until the pit turns red, and then move to the next one.

It's important to get a few points ahead of Quentin as soon as possible, as he'll likely have at least two or three convicts to drop off after the last of them has been captured. There's nothing Spider-Man can do at this point except hope that he has enough points or that Quentin drops them into the wrong pit. Because it takes him a while to get positioned above the pit, the light will occasionally turn from green to red just as he's about to release his quarry.

STEALING A PRISONER

It won't happen often, but occasionally one of Quentin Beck's captured convicts will land on the small circular platform in the center of the pit.

HOLD (B) AND (Y) TO REEL ENEMIES INTO YOUR GRASP

If Spider-Man acts quickly, he can reel in this convict before he falls in, thereby stealing a point from Quentin. Unfortunately, Quentin also tries to employ this tactic, so be extra careful tossing convicts into the pit when he's nearby!

TIEBREAKER

It's not a common occurrence, but there is a chance that Spider-Man and Quentin Beck have an equal number of points after three rounds. In this case, a fourth round will be played with the winner being the quickest one to capture four convicts.

TIE GAME! FIRST CONTESTANT TO SCORE FOUR POINTS WINS.

HOLD (Y) AND (B) TO REEL ENEMIES INTO YOUR GRASP

HOLD (Y) AND (B) TO REEL ENEMIES INTO YOUR GRASP

THE OBSTACLE COURSE

The second portion of this two-event contest is an elaborate obstacle course. Spider-Man must navigate a series of platforms to reach each of the checkpoints. Once each checkpoint is activated (press the Attack Button) a panel slides into position alongside the next row of moving panels. The catch is that Quentin Beck fires energy blasts from his power cannon; Spider-Man must reach the course's end before Quentin hits him three times. Fortunately for Spider-Man, he can use the platforms as cover and make it to far end of the course without suffering the indignity of losing to Quentin.

SIX FINISH LINES

The best way to approach the obstacle course is to think of each checkpoint (marked by a blue Destination Marker) as its own finish line. Each of these "finish lines" provides cover for Spider-Man and a chance to take a breather and study the upcoming segment.

The course's first segment features a lengthy wall of platforms that drop into the floor one-by-one, thereby providing Quentin with a clean shot at Spider-Man. The key is to hold the Sprint Button and run to the first checkpoint quickly enough to remain behind the cover of the upright panels. Hit the marker and patiently ride the platform to the course's second row.

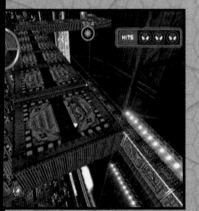

The next segment challenges Spider-Man's ability to Wall Crawl. Wait for the platform to stop, grab onto the upright portion of the wall, and crawl onto the vertical panel to the left. Some of the panels slide back and forth across gaps in the series, so wait for them to abut Spider-Man's panel and then crawl onto them. Continue crawling across the panels slowly and carefully to reach the second checkpoint.

Next up is a very straightforward Wall Crawl from left to right. Each panel is L-shaped. So long as Spider-Man keeps to the upright portion, he won't fall through the horizontal panels when they spin over. Continue crawling to the end of the segment and press the switch at the checkpoint to proceed to the fourth row.

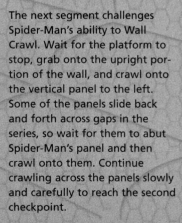

The fourth segment is another exercise in patience. Every other panel spins in unison. Spider-Man must keep off of the panels as they spin, else he'll be a sitting duck for Quentin. Wall Crawl onto the row of panels and carefully move from one panel to the next after each one spins over. There is a brief moment between spins that allows Spider-Man to dismount his current panel before it spins. Consider holding the Sprint Button while crawling to help keep Spider-Man safe.

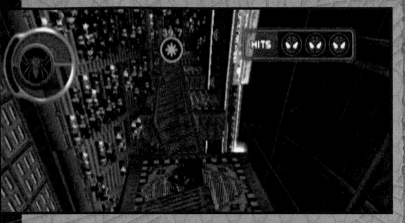

The next segment is another test of Spider-Man's Wall Crawling abilities. This time, the various panels move up and down past one another. Spider-Man must quickly crawl from one to the other during the brief moment that they are aligned. Hold the Sprint Button at all times and dash across the seams between the panels as they move together.

The sixth and final segment is the toughest yet and, unlike the previous ones, Spider-Man can let things fly. The numerous L-shaped platforms are constantly in motion. The row between Spider-Man's starting position and the final checkpoint switch face away from Quentin and are safe, but they quickly spin around to face Quentin when they move to the back row. Carefully jump right to left from platform to platform toward the final Destination Marker. Hit the switch to declare victory over Quentin Beck.

SPIDER-MAN'S FREE TIME

When Spider-Man finishes the contest against Quentin Beck, he still has 1,500 Hero Points to earn before the chapter concludes. Since the Daily Bugle is so close, this is a prime time to see what photo assignments Robbie has to offer. Spider-Man earns 750 Hero Points for the first set of photos that Jameson approves, and this increases by 250 points for every photo mission thereafter, so this is undoubtedly a great way to meet the second To-Do List requirement.

PHOTO MISSIONS

Photo Missions get pretty difficult before long, so if Robbie's deadline for the third or fourth assignment proves to be too tight, remember that they get easier with each successive Hero Upgrade. Be sure to read all about Photo Missions in this guide's The Hero's Work is Never Done chapter.

CHAPTER WRAP-UP

QUENTIN BECK HAD SOME NERVE THINKING THAT SPIDER-MAN WAS A FAKE. ALTHOUGH IT WAS GREAT TO SEE HIM EMBARRASS HIMSELF AFTER THE OBSTACLE COURSE, IT MAY HAVE COME AT A HEAVY PRICE. ONE OF THE CONVICTS SNEAKED OUT OF THE ARENA WHILE SPIDER-MAN WAS PREOCCUPIED. HOPEFULLY IT WASN'T ANYONE WITH A VENDETTA.

CHAPTER 6:

Sugar and Spice

To-Do List

- Go to Doctor Octavius's Apartment.
- Buy Level 4 Swing Upgrade from Store.
- Earn 3000 More Hero Points.

Mission Objectives

Pride of Octavius
Diamonds Miss Play
Cat Thief

State of the Story

Peter's interests in science aren't going by the wayside just because he moonlights as Spider-Man. Today he'll spend dinner with his idol Doctor Otto Octavius in hopes of learning more about his phenomenal research. Hopefully, for Peter's sake, he doesn't forget that Mary Jane's play is tonight as well.

PRIDE OF OCTAVIUS

MISSION TYPE
Swing-To

CHARACTERS INVOLVED
Spider-Man
Peter Parker
Dr. Octavius
Rosie Octavius

Doctor Octavius and his wife were true to their word and have invited Peter to their apartment for dinner. Follow the white Destination Marker to the western side of Central Park where Dr. Octavius's apartment is. Locate the Change Icon atop the building's roof to don Peter's normal attire. Peter gets to listen to the doctor's wonderful theories over dinner but returns to the rooftop before long.

DIAMONDS MISS PLAY

MISSION TYPE
Swing-To
Battle
Car Chase

CHARACTERS SHOWN
Spider-Man
Diamond Thieves
Black Cat
Mary Jane
John Jameson

Spider-Man suddenly remembers that he was supposed to be at Mary Jane's play tonight. The play starts in 3:20 and is all the way downtown in the heart of the Theatre District. Spider-Man doesn't have any time to waste, so get swinging!

Put those Swing Speed Upgrades to use by Web Swinging south through the Lower West Side as fast as possible. Cut on an angle through the major intersection toward the playhouse in the Theatre District.

A huge explosion shatters Spider-Man's concentration just as he nears the theatre. Thieves have blown their way into a nearby diamond store and are making off with a wealth of fine gems. Mary Jane will be mad, but there's nothing Spider-Man can do—he has to go after the crooks!

The blue Destination Marker automatically shifts from the theatre to the diamond store so continue following its direction. Several crooks are on the street, but Spider-Man's first move must be to neutralize the sniper on the roof across the street. Leap onto the rooftop and perform a Sprint Uppercut to knock the gunman into the air. Hold the Attack Button to follow him into the air and then pummel him into unconsciousness.

With the sniper threat resolved, Spider-Man can turn his attention to the crooks on the ground. Web Tie as many of the crooks as possible to minimize the threat of being bum rushed, and then start beating up each of the others one at a time. Be quick to press the Grab Button to dodge their attacks, and immediately launch into counterattacks to keep them off-balance.

The battle isn't over when you've dealt with the last of the thugs near the store. Three more crooks get away in a pickup truck, and one of them is in the back with another sniper rifle! Chase the getaway vehicle by Web Swinging and Web Zipping toward it. Close on them and launch Spider-Man directly into an attack on the gunman in the truckbed—eliminating him is the first step toward stopping the truck! Knock him out of the truck and then beat him into submission before continuing after the driver.

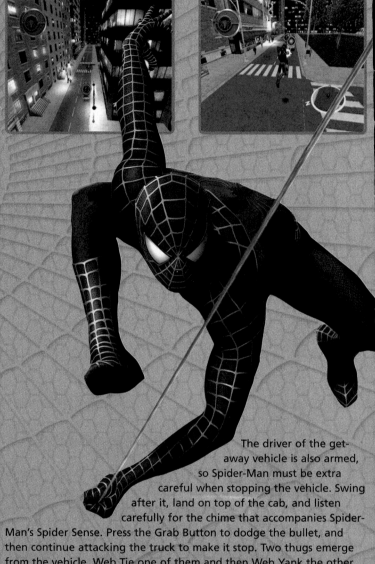

The driver of the getaway vehicle is also armed, so Spider-Man must be extra careful when stopping the vehicle. Swing after it, land on top of the cab, and listen carefully for the chime that accompanies Spider-Man's Spider Sense. Press the Grab Button to dodge the bullet, and then continue attacking the truck to make it stop. Two thugs emerge from the vehicle. Web Tie one of them and then Web Yank the other into the air where he can be easily beaten.

The original blue Destination Marker reappears on the screen as soon as you defeat the last thug in the truck. If Spider-Man hurries he might be able to make it to Mary Jane's play after all! Web Swing through the Theatre District to the alley behind the playhouse.

Spider-Man arrives at the theatre's exit just in time to see Mary Jane being given a bouquet of flowers from an admirer. Could this be the guy she said she was seeing? Is he related to Mr. Jameson at the Daily Bugle? Fortunately for Spider-Man, he isn't given much time to dwell on these questions as Black Cat comes to pay him a visit.

CAT THIEF

MISSION TYPE
Chase
Battle

CHARACTERS INVOLVED
Spider-Man
Black Cat
Art Thieves

Black Cat shows up by surprise and again tempts Spider-Man into chasing her. She has some insight into the art thieves that Spider-Man previously thwarted. She's willing to help him, once she's done teasing him for spying on Mary Jane.

CATCH ME IF YOU CAN

This chase is more difficult than the previous ones because Black Cat doesn't just stick to the rooftops. She slides along the sides of buildings and leaps around corners to evade pursuit. Spider-Man shouldn't have a ton of trouble keeping up with her, but he will have to use his Web Swing, along with the Web Zip and charged jumps that he relied on in the past.

DYNAMIC DUO?

Black Cat stops several times during the chase to flirt with Spider-Man, so don't relax until both of them arrive at the scene of the burglary in the West Village. Multiple thieves are loading priceless art into the back of a truck. They are highly armed and dangerous, but Spider-Man isn't alone in fighting them; Black Cat fights alongside Spider-Man this time!

This is definitely the toughest fight so far, so Spider-Man must take care to ensure he comes out in one piece. Not only are there several guards, but two of them also have machine guns. Successfully defeating these crooks requires constant motion on Spider-Man's part, and generous use of his Spider Reflexes.

Drop off the building's edge to start the fight, and quickly Sprint Uppercut one of the thugs near the truck. Black Cat joins the fray, and although she can definitely hold her own against these thugs, Spider-Man shouldn't rely on her too much. Dodge as many attacks as possible, and launch a barrage of counterattacks to soften up the thug horde.

Activate Spider Reflexes as soon as the gunfire starts, and repeatedly tap the Grab Button to dodge the automatic weapons' bullets. The thug eventually stops firing to reload—that's Spider-Man's chance to yank the gun out of his hand with a tap of the Web Button! Actively dodge as many attacks as possible to refill the Spider Reflexes Meter, and then use them to gain an edge on the enemies.

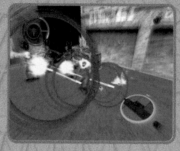

Despite their great teamwork, Spider-Man finds himself alone at the end of the fight; Black Cat is nowhere to be found. She ran off with the golden statue while he was taking care of the last thug!

SPIDER-MAN'S FREE TIME

Each of the missions in this chapter paid hefty Hero Points rewards, so Spider-Man shouldn't have much more than 500 Hero Points to earn before reaching the requirement. Head north toward the Upgrade Store near the Daily Bugle, and purchase the Swing Speed Level 4 upgrade. Spider-Man should also have enough Hero Points to acquire the following Hero Upgrades: The Hero Punch, Level 4 Air Combo, and the Interceptor Kick.

When you exit the store, look for pedestrians with Voluntary Missions to offer. With a bit of luck, Spider-Man might find himself foiling the plans of brazen armed criminals—the riskier the Voluntary Mission, the bigger the Hero Points reward! Those who have been following closely should gain the "Hero in Training" award near the end of this chapter for eclipsing the 15,000 mark in total Hero Points earned. Good job!

CHAPTER WRAP-UP

POOR PETER WANTED TO SEE MARY JANE'S PLAY, BUT HIS RESPONSIBILI-TIES TO THE PEOPLE OF NEW YORK INTERFERED ONCE AGAIN. AT LEAST BLACK CAT CAME BY TO CHEER HIM UP. OR DID SHE? COULD IT BE THAT SHE NEEDED SPIDER-MAN'S HELP IN FIGHTING THOSE ART THIEVES SO SHE COULD GET THE GOLDEN STATUE? EVERY DAY YIELDS MORE QUES-TIONS THAN ANSWERS WHEN YOU'RE A SUPERHERO.

CHAPTER 5:

When Aliens Attack

To-Do List

🕸 Complete the Daily Bugle Assignment.

Mission Objectives

Mysterio Exposed
War of the Worlds
Mysterio Madness

State of the Story

It's been a while since Mr. Jameson brought up that whacko Quentin Beck, but that's about to change. Apparently, Spider-Man was the only one who realized that Quentin Beck was a phony, because now he's trying to organize a press conference.

MYSTERIO EXPOSED

MISSION TYPE

Swing-To
Rescue

CHARACTERS INVOLVED

Spider-Man
Mr. Jameson
Mysterio
Reporters

CHINATOWN

It's been a while since Peter last checked in with Mr. Jameson at the Daily Bugle to see if there are any assignments for him. Follow the white Destination Marker to the Daily Bugle's roof and enter through the ventilation system. Peter will change back into his work clothes automatically and go talk to Mr. Jameson.

It turns out that Mr. Jameson was hoping Peter would visit. Quentin Beck has called for a press conference to discuss Spider-Man, and Peter must race over there to photograph the event before it's over.

While Peter and Mr. Jameson were talking, the super villain Mysterio revealed himself to the audience at the conference. Although his threats were met with jeers and laughter, nobody was laughing when his robot flyers began firing lasers into the crowd. The reporters are trapped and the old theatre is slowly starting to catch fire. Spider-Man has 1:30 to reach the theatre if he's to have any chance of saving the reporters!

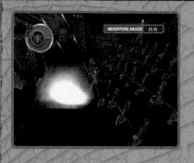

ROBOTS BEWARE!

Spider-Man will be constantly on the move as he rescues the first two reporters, so the robots hovering about the theatre shouldn't pose much of a threat—they're only dangerous when Spider-Man stands still. Don't worry about attacking them until after the first reporters are safe.

CANNONBALL KICK

If Spider-Man has already purchased the Cannonball Kick Hero Upgrade, he can easily fend off the robot flyers with a tap of the Attack Button as he swings through the air. It will take two Cannonball Kicks to defeat a robot flyer. Use the Lock-On camera to help guide Spider-Man's attacks (Down on the d-pad).

The theatre where the conference is being held is located in Chinatown. Web Swing south through Soho, along the main avenue that leads away from the Daily Bugle, to Chinatown. Run through the theatre doors and ascend the stairs to the uppermost balcony area. Once there, Spider-Man realizes that the main theatre area is engulfed in flames and six reporters will die if he doesn't act fast. He has to ignore Mysterio for the time being and save the two reporters dangling from the balconies!

Three reporters are on the stage, cowering in the corner behind the Mysterio hologram—they are safe for now. Spider-Man's first task is to rescue the two reporters dangling from the balcony; he has only 1:00 to do it! Run and leap from the rear balcony to the one on the right-hand side, and press the Web Button to reel in the reporter. Approach the edge of the balcony facing away from the stage and charge the Jump Meter. Leap toward the rear balcony (where Spider-Man entered) and Web Swing over to it. Press any button to put down the reporter. Now, repeat these tactics to save the reporter on the left balcony.

The countdown timer stops once the first two reporters are safe. Now it's time to rescue the other four reporters, one of which is on the right-hand balcony. Save him, and then run and leap down onto the main stage to tend to the remaining three. Take a moment to destroy any robot flyers that might be nearby. It takes only three quick punches and kicks to destroy one of Mysterio's robot flyers; the fewer there are shooting at Spider-Man, the better off he'll be. When attacking the robots in midair, use the Lock-On camera (Down on the d-pad) to help guide Spider-Man's attacks.

Reel in one of the reporters and stand near the back of the stage, facing the balcony. It's a long way there, and with the entire floor on fire, Spider-Man has to be extra careful. The best way to guarantee that he and the reporter reach the balcony safely is to fully charge the Jump Meter and leap high and straight into the air. Throw a Web Line to the ceiling and hold the Sprint Button to get a Swing Boost. Jump from the peak of the swing to land on the balcony. Continue moving back and forth from the balcony to the stage until all of the remaining reporters are safe.

With the reporters evacuated, Spider-Man's focus can shift to the remaining robot flyers. Return to the stage to finish destroying any that happen to fly within range, but avoid leaping out too far over the fiery floor. Leap and Web Swing back up to either of the side balconies to see if the stragglers will swoop by. If necessary, leap from one of the balconies toward the robot, and perform an air combo attack to destroy it. Quickly throw a Web Line before falling into the flames, and swing back to solid ground.

Once all of the reporters have been saved and the robot flyers destroyed, the Mysterio hologram will warn Spider-Man of the impending alien invasion. His army has already laid siege to the Statue of Liberty and if Spider-Man doesn't stop him, all of New York City will fall.

WAR OF THE WORLDS

MISSION TYPE
Swing-To
Combat Puzzle

CHARACTERS INVOLVED
Spider-Man
Mysterio

Web Swing through the city to the southern tip, where the Statue of Liberty can be seen. Approach the blue Destination Marker to have Spider-Man survey the situation.

Mysterio's Mothership has landed atop the Statue of Liberty and is casting a powerful energy shield around it. Worse yet, this extraterrestrial super villain has cloaked Lady Liberty with a hologram in his image. Dozens of UFOs are hovering between Liberty Island and the Manhattan waterfront, so finally Spider-Man has a way to reach the mothership: Spider-Man must Web Swing across the harbor by shooting Web Lines to the underside of each UFO.

Leap high into the air and Web Swing from the nearest UFO. Hold the Sprint Button as you Web Swing to get the necessary Swing Boost, and also charge the Jump Meter. Leap as high and far into the air as possible, and then shoot another Web Line to continue Web Swinging. Spider-Man doesn't have to swing from each and every UFO, but if he tries to skip more than one, he will likely end up splashing into the water below. Carefully follow the path of UFOs to the Statue of Liberty's base.

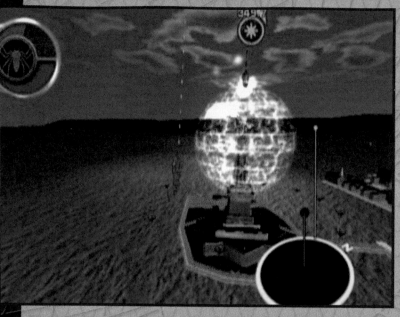

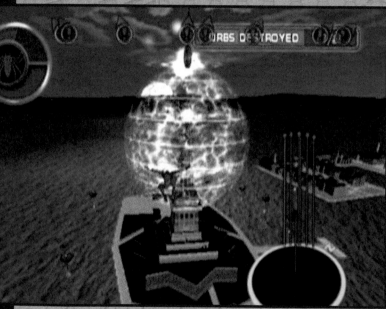

There are a number of UFOs hovering low to the ground around the island's perimeter. Leap into the air and Web Swing from one of these UFOs. Get as much of a Swing Boost as possible to send Spider-Man flying straight up into the air. He can then attach a Web Line to one of the antennae that holds an orb.

The mothership slowly rotates in a counter-clockwise fashion atop the statue. In order to keep up with the orbs at the end of the antennae, Spider-Man should Web Swing in a *clockwise* direction. This helps ensure that his Web Lines are short and taught, which keeps him at the necessary height and speed.

Web Swing outward, toward each of the orbs one at a time. Leap from the Web Line and press the Attack Button to destroy the orb. Use the Lock-On camera (Down on the d-pad). It takes only one hit to destroy an orb. Continue Web Swinging round and round the mothership until you've destroyed all 8 orbs.

The mothership's nerve center becomes accessible for a brief period after all 8 orbs are destroyed. Quickly Web Swing onto the central area, avoid the slowly moving fan blade, and jump up to attack the target in the center to destroy the mothership.

SWING SPEED REQUIREMENTS

This mission can be made considerably easier with the Swing Speed Level 5 upgrade. It really increases the distance Spider-Man travels through the air when jumping between swings. It is possible to complete this objective with Swing Speed Level 3, but those with level 3 or lower should definitely consider visiting the nearby Upgrade Store before trying to save this important monument.

Once safely on Liberty Island, the Mini Map will show 8 orbs as targets. These orbs are positioned on the ends of the mothership's outstretched antennae and are the source of the craft's power. Spider-Man must Web Swing to the top of the statue and destroy each of the orbs. Only then will he be able to access the central control and destroy the force field.

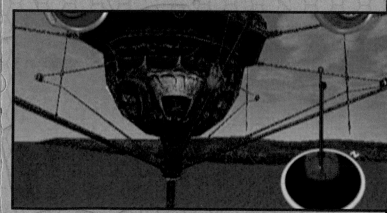

Mysterio's voice calls out to Spider-Man once again, this time inviting him to Mysterio's hidden fortress. Spider-Man hops aboard one of the boats in the harbor and cruises back to the Financial District.

MYSTERIO MADNESS

MISSION TYPE
Swing-To
Combat Puzzle

CHARACTERS INVOLVED
Spider-Man
Mysterio
Hop-N-Hacks
Distorted Spider-Men

It's time for Spider-Man to accept Mysterio's invitation. Follow the blue Destination Marker north from the Financial District, past Chinatown, and uptown toward the apartment building with the open window. Crawl through the window to enter what appears to be a very typical bedroom. A second blue Destination Marker appears near the bookcase; go to it to reveal a secret entrance to Mysterio's lair.

FUNHOUSE ENTRANCE

The secret elevator delivers Spider-Man to the entrance of Mysterio's funhouse-inspired fortress. Before Spider-Man can gain admittance, he must first prove himself against a Hop-N-Hack.

CHILD'S PLAY?

Hop-N-Hacks are essentially inflatable, wobbly, bouncy toys with razor-sharp cleavers in their hands. They are quite resilient and have the nasty habit of bouncing back to quickly counterattack after being hit. The key to defeating one is to attack, then immediately press the Grab Button to dodge its incoming counterattack, and then quickly perform a follow-up attack.

Mysterio's first test consists of a solitary Hop-N-Hack. Attack fast and keep moving to avoid its cleaver. Watch for its bounces and be ready to dodge any counterattacks it attempts, else Spider-Man will certainly lose considerable health. The door in the clown's mouth opens once the Hop-N-Hack is defeated. Step into the funhouse.

UPSIDE-DOWN ROOM

The first area inside the "House of Laughs" is a fashionable dining room that gets turned upside-down just as three Hop-N-Hacks appear. The bouncing baddies try very hard to surround Spider-Man, so he must try equally hard to isolate them one at a time.

Although it's difficult to Web Yank a Hop-N-Hack while it's on the ground, it can be done if Spider-Man catches it mid-bounce. Use the Web Yank to separate one from the other two, and then rush toward it. Hit it with an attack, and then quickly dodge and counterattack to dish out some damage. Try dodging away from the Hop-N-Hack so that Spider-Man can counter with the Counter Flip Kick. Doing so will get the Hop-N-Hack off the ground and make it susceptible to additional attacks, without the fear of a bounce-back counterattack.

SMACK 'EM IN THE BACK

Of course, Spider-Man is much more maneuverable than these playful meat cleavers. Put his agility to use by leaping up and over the Hop-N-Hacks to get a clean attack at its backside. Spider-Man can prevent a counterattack if he strikes the Hop-N-Hack in the back. Also, don't be afraid to use those Spider Reflexes, as they can really come in handy when trying to time a counterattack.

Spider-Man regains some health once the third and final Hop-N-Hack is deflated. Although the room doesn't rotate back to its normal orientation, a door leading to the next hallway opens and a blue Destination Marker appears. Leap up to the door and drop through the chute in the floor to enter the next area of this complex fortress.

HALL OF MIRRORS

The Hall of Mirrors is a circular room lined with dozens of funhouse mirrors, which is a little ironic, because the horrors of this room are nothing to laugh at. Each time Spider-Man approaches a mirror, a Distorted Spider-Man emerges from the glass to attack. These malformed clones don't have all of Spider-Man's special abilities, but they can perform Web Yanks and can deliver a sufficient beating with a barrage of punches and kicks.

There's more to the room than just the Distorted Spider-Men. Every third mirror hides a projector. When all of the projectors are allowed to shine on the orb in the center of the room, the doorway leading to Mysterio's Control Room opens. The key is to quickly break a few mirrors and note the location of the first projector. Then swiftly run around the room, breaking every third mirror, avoiding the Distorted Spider-Men as you go. This is not as easy as it sounds.

Keep moving and be ready to hit the Grab Button the instant Spider-Man's head flashes to dodge incoming attacks. Use the Earth Breaker Punch and Multi-Web Tie abilities to keep the Distorted Spider-Men at bay. Keep a close count on the mirrors, and perform a Sprint Uppercut on every third one to quickly break the glass and reveal the projector behind it.

AVOIDING THE WEB YANK

It's not every day that Spider-Man has to avoid Web Yank attacks, but he will when he faces the Distorted Spider-Men.

When all of the projectors are able to shine directly on the glass-encased head in the room's center, a beam of light burns an exit for Spider-Man. Leave the Hall of Mirrors through this opening.

MYSTERIO'S CONTROL ROOM

As luck would have it, Mysterio wasn't actually in the Control Room, after all. Spider-Man survived the dangers of the funhouse to discover that Mysterio had simply left behind another hologram. Follow the blue Destination Marker out of the Control Room, back to the bedroom and, ultimately, back outside through the window.

SPIDER-MAN'S FREE TIME

Spider-Man earns a large number of Hero Points through the course of this chapter, and he should spend them on every available Hero Upgrade as soon as he exits Mysterio's secret fortress. The Swing Speed Upgrades will make completing many of the various Challenges that much easier.

The next destination is uptown on the Upper West Side, so start traveling in that direction while completing as many Voluntary Missions as possible. Also, try to find some of the Secret and Skyscraper Tokens—they're a great source of Hero Points and they help increase the completion percentage on the Game Status screen.

CHAPTER WRAP-UP

SPIDER-MAN HAD QUITE A DAY TODAY, AND IT ALL BEGAN WITH AN INNOCENT VISIT TO THE DAILY BUGLE. NOT ONLY DID HE RESCUE HALF A DOZEN REPORTERS FROM A BURNING THEATRE, BUT HE ALSO SAVED THE PEOPLE OF NEW YORK CITY FROM AN ALIEN INVASION! LAST BUT NOT LEAST, HE SURVIVED A TRIP THROUGH MYSTERIO'S FUNHOUSE-INSPIRED FORTRESS, ONLY TO FIND THAT MYSTERIO WAS ONCE AGAIN NOT WHERE SPIDER-MAN THOUGHT HE WAS. THE CONSTANT USE OF HOLOGRAMS CAN'T LAST FOREVER—MYSTERIO WILL MEET HIS MATCH ONE DAY!

BACK TO LIBERTY ISLAND!

There are three Challenges and three Secret Tokens on Ellis Island and Liberty Island that will necessitate a return trip later. There are two helicopters that fly between the southern tip of Manhattan (near the FC) and Ellis Island. Shoot a Web Line to the first 'copter, and then transition to the second one as they pass each other over the water. There is a third helicopter that flies back and forth between Ellis Island and the Statue of Liberty. Web Swing from this third 'copter to reach Lady Liberty!

When Good Men Go Bad

To-Do List

- Buy Level 5 Swing Upgrade from Store.
- Earn 3000 More Hero Points.

Mission Objectives

Death of Octavius
Check on Dr. Connors
Swing by the Daily Bugle

State of the Story

It's now painfully obvious to Spider-Man that Quentin Beck was just one of Mysterio's pawns and, for whatever reason, Mysterio is determined to destroy both Spider-Man and his wonderful city. The last thing Spider-Man needs to deal with is another super villain on the loose. At least he can put his worries aside for a few hours and attend Doctor Otto Octavius's unveiling...

DEATH OF OCTAVIUS

MISSION TYPE
Swing-To
Action Puzzle

CHARACTERS INVOLVED
Spider-Man
Doctor Octavius
Rosie Octavius
Dr. Connors
Dignitaries
Harry Osborn

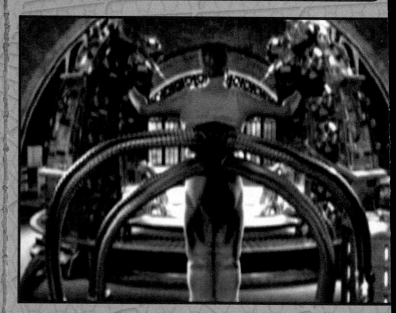

SPOILER WARNING!

This chapter contains several climactic moments in the story of *Spider-Man 2: The Movie*. Those who wish to be surprised should refrain from reading ahead until the in-game cinematics play out. This applies doubly to those who have not yet seen the movie and are unaware of the fate that befalls Doctor Octavius.

Spider-Man remembers that tonight is the night Doctor Octavius plans to unveil his reactor. Follow the blue Destination Marker to Doctor Octavius's apartment in the Upper West Side, overlooking Central Park. There is a Change Icon on the roof that Spider-Man can access to turn back to Peter Parker.

Although the presentation starts out according to plan, the inhibitor chips in the reactor soon malfunction and a tragic accident ensues. The reactor grows increasingly unstable and, before long, Rosie Octavius is struck dead by a powerful blast of energy. During the commotion, Peter runs to don his costume and comes crashing through the windows as Spider-Man just in time to see Doctor Octavius get knocked to the ground.

There are four control terminals that must be destroyed in order to shut down the reactor before the situation becomes ever more dire. The room is shaped like a "+" and there is a control terminal on each of the reactor's four sides. Although it takes only one quick kick or punch to destroy each terminal, getting to them isn't quite as simple. The reactor creates a pulsing energy sphere that erratically shifts inward and outward from the reactor's center. This energy sphere is not only impenetrable but it also delivers significant damage to Spider-Man if he touches it—not to mention the fact that he'll be tossed like a ragdoll into the corner of the room. If Spider-Man is to deactivate the reactor, he must move quickly from one side of the room to the other to avoid the pulsing energy sphere. Unfortunately for Spider-Man, the pulsing becomes more erratic with the destruction of each terminal.

When you begin this mission, stand back for a second and allow the sphere to expand to its widest point before you move to destroy the nearby terminal; doing so will help you avoid being hit. Watch for the sphere to contract, then run and dive for the terminal on either the right or left. Slowly work around the room, taking out each of the control terminals while trying to avoid the energy sphere and the stray energy blasts. Beware that that the sphere gets very erratic after you've destroyed the third terminal. It will expand outward twice before fully contracting to its smallest diameter, so choose when to make your move wisely.

Spider-Man knows that there are a lot of people who would love to blame him for this catastrophe, so he's forced to flee the scene after powering down the reactor. Hopefully Doctor Octavius is all right! In the meantime, there is an Upgrade Store directly across Central Park from Doctor Octavius's apartment, and that is where Spider-Man should go. Web Zip through the trees in the south end of the park and visit the store on the Upper East Side. Purchase the Level 5 Swing Speed Upgrade and as many of the other new upgrades as possible, especially the Whirlwind Kick and the Stair Step Kicks Combo.

STRAY BLASTS OF ENERGY

The pulsing energy sphere isn't the only threat to Spider-Man's health. Stray energy occasionally strikes out from the reactor with deadly force. Watch for Spider-Man's head to flash, and then quickly press the Grab Button to dodge the incoming energy blast. These blasts occur roughly every 10 seconds, so be ready for them.

The control terminals have a blinking red light and are located just out of the energy sphere's reach. The dangerous part of this mission is trying to get from one terminal to the other. Stand back and watch for a pattern to the energy sphere's pulsing. The sphere shifts between three diameters. Watch for it to shift from its widest size to the middle diameter and then back to the smallest diameter. Make a running leap into the next area of the room as soon as it tightens up. There is no time limit, so take some time to watch for a pattern and then make the move.

UPGRADES STORE

HERO UPGRADE
STAIR STEP KICKS COMBO
NOT ACQUIRED

COSTS 1200 POINTS

(X), (X), (A) THEN PRESS (X) RAPIDLY EXECUTE MANY KICKS ON THE ENEMY. ONLY DURING SPIDER REFLEXES (MUST FIRST PURCHASE JAW LAUNCHER)

CURRENT HERO POINTS   39596

SELECT ITEM FROM ABOVE FOR INFORMATION AND IF AVAILABLE TO PURCHASE.

◆◆ MOVE (C) (B) RESUME (A) PURCHASE

CHECK ON DR. CONNORS

MISSION TYPE
Swing-To
Combat

CHARACTERS INVOLVED
Spider-Man
Peter Parker
Mysterio's Flying Robots
Dr. Connors
Doctor Octavius

Spider-Man realizes that he needs to visit Dr. Connors. A blue Destination Marker appears, leading Spider-Man back across Central Park toward the university near the Gramercy neighborhood. Web Swing through the city in the direction of Dr. Connor's office at the college.

Just as Spider-Man gets about halfway to Dr. Connors's office, a small contingent of Mysterio's Flying Robots swoops down and attacks. Try to remain atop a rooftop to fight them without any obstructions. Watch for Spider-Man's head to flash, and press the Grab Button to dodge laser fire. Take on each of the Flying Robots one at a time, using quick air combo attacks to defeat them.

While Spider-Man was battling Mysterio's Flying Robots, Doctor Octavius was coincidentally paying his old buddy Dr. Connors a visit. The two get into a heated argument and Doctor Octavius, overwhelmed by the loss of his wife Rosie, decides that he will use his newfound power to fund his endeavors through criminal activity. He throws Dr. Connors to the ground and leaves the lab, still wearing his tentacle suit.

Continue the trip to the campus. Approach the door to Dr. Connors' building to change back to Peter Parker. Peter finds his professor lying on the floor of his lab. Although Peter can't understand why Dr. Connors would mumble the words he does, he wastes no time in rushing him to the hospital.

SWING BY THE DAILY BUGLE

MISSION TYPE
Swing-To

CHARACTERS INVOLVED
Spider-Man
Peter Parker
Mr. Jameson
Robbie Robertson

Spider-Man is having a tough time figuring out what his next move should be, so he decides to head to the Daily Bugle. Not only might Mr. Jameson know something about Doc Ock, but Peter just might be able to make some extra money too!

Follow the blue Destination Marker south through the city, to the Daily Bugle offices in Midtown. Mr. Jameson and Robbie are in a meeting when Peter arrives, but he arrives in time to hear Mr. Jameson refer to "Doc Ock." And of course, he'd love some pictures of the city's newest super villain.

SPIDER-MAN'S FREE TIME

The various missions in this chapter will give Spider-Man nearly all of the Hero Points he needs to complete the To-Do List requirement. Spend a few minutes assisting the citizens in distress in the middle of the city to earn the remainder of the Hero Points necessary to fulfill the Award requirements listed on the Game Status screen.

CHAPTER WRAP-UP

SPIDER-MAN SPENT A LOT OF TIME IN THIS CHAPTER WEB SWINGING BACK AND FORTH ACROSS THE CITY, BUT IT WASN'T WITHOUT MAKING SOME SERIOUS HEADWAY IN THE STORY. NOT ONLY HAS HIS NEXT MAJOR ADVERSARY BEEN REVEALED, BUT HE ALSO GOT THE CHANCE TO PURCHASE SEVERAL NEW HERO UPGRADES.

CHAPTER 11:

The Underworld of Crime

To-Do List

- Meet Aunt May at the Bank.
- Earn 4000 More Hero Points.

Mission Objectives

Doc Ock Bank
Rescue Aunt May

State of the Story

Yesterday was a tragic and confusing day for Spider-Man. Not only did the wife of his mentor die during an experiment gone awry, but the good Doctor Octavius has, if the rumors are true, seemingly lost his mind and turned into the next super villain! And to make matters worse, Dr. Connors has suffered a suspicious injury and is hospitalized. This is enough to make Mysterio's alien invasion seem ordinary!

DOC OCK BANK

MISSION TYPE
Swing-To
Combat
Rescue

CHARACTERS INVOLVED
Spider-Man
Peter Parker
Aunt May
Doc Ock
Ock Thugs

Mr. Jameson doesn't have any specific assignments for Peter at the moment, but the thought of earning some money is enough to remind Peter that he has to meet his Aunt May at the bank. The bank is located in the Upper East Side, and a white Destination Marker appears on-screen to lead the way. A large, blue square with a star in the center of it appears on the Zoom Map to help guide the way. A blue Destination Marker appears as soon as Spider-Man arrives at the bank entrance. Scale the wall to the ledge above to find the Change Icon.

Peter joins his Aunt May outside the bank, and together they go inside to keep their appointment with the banker. However, Doc Ock and his Ock Thugs interrupt their meeting. Peter appears to run and hide, but we know where he's really going: to change into Spider-Man!

Doc Ock and Ock Thugs

BOSS BATTLE: DOC OCK AND OCK THUGS

BOSS ATTACK	DAMAGE TO SPIDER-MAN
Tentacle Claw	Low
Tentacle Throw	Low
Tentacle Slam	Moderate
Ock Thug Explosive	Moderate

Spider-Man must face off against Doc Ock and his crew in order to protect the bank's patrons, and especially Aunt May. Each Ock Thug has a large, bladed gun that can fire explosive charges. Watch for the explosive orbs that get lobbed at Spider-Man, and move away from them before they detonate.

Doc Ock lashes out with his tentacles, but Spider-Man senses the attack and his head flashes. Quickly press the Grab Button to dodge the attack. Then immediately tap the Web Button to counterattack with a Web Line that binds the tentacle to the ground for a short period. This gives Spider-Man time to deal with the Ock Thugs.

Web Trap one of the Ock Thugs, and then take on the other two simultaneously, using the various attacks that Spider-Man purchased from the Upgrade Store. The Air Pile Driver and Jaw Launcher attacks are especially useful against Doc Ock's cronies.

Once the first wave of Ock Thugs is incapacitated, Doc Ock attacks with increased aggression. Stand a few steps back from him and watch for one of his tentacles to flash yellow. Be ready to dodge, counter with a web attack to bind the tentacle, and then rush in to deliver a combo. Doc Ock starts to use his tentacles to move along the room's wall. When he does this, Spider-Man has to leap into the air to attack him. Don't be afraid to get in his face and attack so long as you're ready to dodge a tentacle attack.

Should Spider-Man start to suffer significant damage, switch to Spider Reflexes and rush toward Doc Ock. Watch for the red rings to appear and dodge his attack, but then use one of the counterattack combos to instantly unload on him. Doc Ock ends the fight and flees once he suffers roughly 20% damage to his health bar. But before he leaves, he decides to grab hold of Aunt May and take her with him.

Doc Ock may have left, but the battle is not yet over! Rush through the door in the corner of the bank to take on another batch of three Ock Thugs. Launch into battle with a Sprint Uppercut while they are still grouped together; this sends each of them flying into the air. Repeatedly tap the Attack Button while Spider-Man's airborne for a lengthy Air Combo. Try to juggle one of the Ock Thugs by pressing the Web Button and Down on the Movement Controls to pull him back up to Spider-Man when he starts to fall.

Keep an eye out for any remaining Ock Thugs, as they fire explosive charges. Immediately leap and grab hold of the ceiling to avoid such blasts. Continue to attack with combos, and keep at least one of the Ock Thugs bound in a Web Trap until there is only one left, and then finish him off.

RESCUE AUNT MAY

Doc Ock is about to flee the bank in a helicopter, and he's taking Aunt May with him! Spider-Man has thirty seconds to make it to the bank's roof—he's got a chopper to catch! Charge the Jump Meter and leap into a Wallsprint up the side of the bank to the rooftop.

CAREFUL, SPIDER-MAN!

Beware the helicopter's spinning blades, as they will cut Spider-Man to shreds should he leap on top of the chopper while its blades are whirling.

Spider-Man is forced to look on in horror as Doc Ock deposits Aunt May on the train tracks in the path of an oncoming train! Spider-Man must sprint and Web Zip past the train to rescue Aunt May before it's too late! There is no margin for error in this task, as the train is bearing down on Aunt May at an alarming rate. Spider-Man cannot risk falling from the tracks or making unnecessary Web Swings or Wall Crawls.

Sprint toward the building's edge and jump as far as possible out over the train. Web Zip past the train, onto the tracks, and immediately tap the Jump Button again while holding the Sprint Button to catapult Spider-Man forward on the tracks. Sprint toward Aunt May to pull her out of harm's way before the train reaches her.

SPIDER-MAN'S FREE TIME

Spider-Man finishes his duties in this chapter with roughly half of the Hero Points required to move on. Fortunately, he'll also end up in the El Barrio neighborhood, an area of the city he's not likely to have visited yet. Consult the 'Hero's Work is Never Done' chapter of this guide for tips on finding the many Secret Tokens, Hideout Tokens, and Buoy Tokens in this area, and then give some of the Challenges a try. The Level 5 Swing Speed Upgrade will make the Challenges rated "Easy" and "Medium" a breeze.

Assuming Spider-Man reaches the rooftop in time, the 'copter takes off as soon as he arrives. Jump off the building and shoot a Web Line to the chopper and hang on. Try to shoot the Web Line when you're close to the helicopter; this will keep the line as short as possible to avoid getting snagged on a building. Doc Ock flies the chopper to the elevated train tracks near El Barrio, and Spider-Man automatically drops onto a nearby rooftop as the chopper begins to land.

CHAPTER WRAP-UP

SPIDER-MAN HAS FOUND A NEW NEMESIS IN DOC OCK, AND THE FEELING IS MUTUAL. IT'S OBVIOUS THAT BATTLING DOC OCK WON'T BE EASY THANKS TO THOSE METAL TENTACLES HE HAS HOLDING HIM DOWN—NOT TO MENTION THE GANG OF CRONIES HE HAS FOLLOWING HIM AROUND! GOOD THING SPIDER-MAN PURCHASED THOSE HERO UPGRADES, ELSE THINGS COULD HAVE TURNED SOUTH IN A HURRY. AUNT MAY IS THANKFUL TOO!

CHAPTER 18:

Shocking Developments

To-Do List

- Go to Your Apartment.
- Earn 4000 More Hero Points.

Mission Objectives

Marriage Proposal
Hello Shocker

State of the Story

Peter Parker came very close to being an orphan, and Doc Ock is going to pay for it! How dare Doc Ock take his Aunt May and place her in front of an oncoming train? Good thing Peter was able to escape the bank and put on his Spider-Man costume in time, else he may have been forced to reveal his powers to the public.

MARRIAGE PROPOSAL

MISSION TYPE

Swing-To

Chase

CHARACTERS INVOLVED

Spider-Man

Black Cat

Spider-Man remembers that there are some things he needs to do back home in his apartment. A white Destination Marker appears on the screen to lead the way. Web Swing south through the city from the El Barrio area to Peter's apartment building in the West Village. Once there, Wallsprint up the building's side to the balcony with the open windows to enter his residence.

Spider-Man checks his answering machine and discovers that Mr. Jameson wants him at his son's banquet immediately. Spider-Man rushes back out into the night sky for fear of being fired (again) if he's late. A blue Destination Marker guides Spider-Man to the building hosting the Jameson's gala in the Gramercy neighborhood. Wallsprint to the building's roof and approach the skylights.

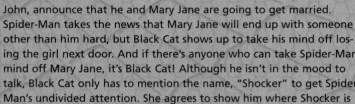

Spider-Man arrives just in time to overhear Mr. Jameson's son, John, announce that he and Mary Jane are going to get married. Spider-Man takes the news that Mary Jane will end up with someone other than him hard, but Black Cat shows up to take his mind off losing the girl next door. And if there's anyone who can take Spider-Man's mind off Mary Jane, it's Black Cat! Although he isn't in the mood to talk, Black Cat only has to mention the name, "Shocker" to get Spider-Man's undivided attention. She agrees to show him where Shocker is hiding out, and the two embark on another chase through the city.

FOLLOWING BLACK CAT

Black Cat leads Spider-Man on a lengthy journey south through the city. She moves at a decent pace, but she follows a relatively straight path and doesn't go out of her way to shake Spider-Man from following her. After all, the two have developed a kinship of sorts thanks to their common "superpowers" bond.

Try to stick to the rooftops of the taller buildings when following Black Cat, as it makes keeping an eye on her easier. Sprint and jump as far and fast as possible, and use the Web Zip technique to catapult Spider-Man in Black Cat's direction. She leads Spider-Man through the campus near Gramercy, toward the waterfront at the Lower East Side. Join her on the ground outside the large warehouse where Shocker is apparently holed up.

HELLO SHOCKER

MISSION TYPE
Boss Battle

CHARACTERS INVOLVED
Spider-Man
Black Cat
Shocker
Shocker Thugs

Black Cat leads Spider-Man to Shocker's whereabouts, as promised. Cross the interior of the warehouse to the large room at the end of the hallway, and prepare to do battle with someone from Spider-Man's past.

Shocker & Shocker Thugs

BOSS BATTLE: SHOCKER & SHOCKER THUGS

BOSS ATTACK	DAMAGE TO SPIDER-MAN
Homing Energy Blast	Low
Large Shockwave Attack	High
Shocker Thug Attack	Moderate

Shocker wields amazing electrical attacks and wears a thickly padded suit to protect him from his high voltage powers. Although Spider-Man often ridicules Shocker's sense of style, his quilted suit does an excellent job of keeping him safe from the electrical blasts he dishes out. Shocker isn't much of a brawler, but that doesn't mean he's a pushover. Not only is he incredibly mobile, he also has several highly shocking attacks that can leave Spider-Man electrocuted and dazed. And when those don't work, he'll call in for reinforcements!

Spider-Man arrives on the scene with Black Cat at his side. She definitely comes in handy during this battle—Black Cat takes care of Shocker's Thugs, leaving Spider-Man to concentrate on Shocker! The room in which the fight takes place has several platforms high on the walls. A couple of lengthy corridors connect the corners of the room. More importantly, however, are the three huge fans in the center of the room that can propel Spider-Man straight up into the air. These make it very easy to Web Zip and Web Swing across the room in a speedy manner.

Unlike previous battles, this one is much more frantic, and it involves a great deal of moving around. Shocker floats around the room throughout the fight, all the while sending electrical volleys toward Spider-Man at a frightening rate. Spider-Man must try to stay as close as possible to Shocker so that he can get in an attack whenever the opportunity arises. It helps to use the Lock-On camera (Down on the d-pad). Of course, keep an eye out for Spider-Man's signature head flash, and quickly press the Grab Button to dodge an incoming homing attack.

Follow the blue Destination Marker around the room, trying to stay as close as possible to it. Shocker occasionally fires a homing energy blast at Spider-Man, but it can be avoided with a timely tap of the Grab Button or by leaping out of the way. If you're close to Shocker, go for the counterattack, and try to link it with a combo to begin dwindling his health reserves.

One way to tell if Shocker's mighty shockwave attack is coming is if the lights briefly flicker off and then back on. It's subtle, so you'll have to pay close attention, but the room momentarily darkens as Shocker draws power to perform this attack. Let this be your cue to get as far away as possible from him!

Shocker occasionally touches down on the ground or on a platform to prepare his massive shockwave attack. If possible, rush forward and deliver a Sprint Uppercut at this very moment to interrupt the attack and exploit his vulnerability in the air. Conversely, Spider-Man must flee to the other side of the room when Shocker extends both his arms out in front of him, as this means he's about to unleash the shockwave.

Success will come so long as you keep moving and go in for the attack only when Shocker's electrical gloves aren't sparking, or when he lands. With some practice, Spider-Man can land Cannonball Kicks on Shocker while Web Swinging through the room. It's also possible to consistently leap away from homing attacks and immediately launch into a counterattack. Lastly, don't be afraid to use Spider Reflexes to pack more pop in each punch!

When Spider-Man finally delivers what he thinks is the knockout blow to Shocker, the super villain musters up enough energy for one final attack. He uses his powers to slam Black Cat into the ceiling. Although she's all right, Spider-Man's instinct to check on her gives Shocker just enough time to escape.

SPIDER-MAN'S FREE TIME

Spider-Man will likely have at least 1000 Hero Points left to earn after defeating Shocker, so take to the streets and search out citizens in distress or petty crimes to solve. Because Spider-Man is already on the Lower East Side, this is a great time to stop by Mary Jane's apartment in Soho to complete a Mary Jane Mission.

At her apartment, Spider-Man finds a message telling him to meet Mary Jane at a specific location. He then has a specific amount of time to reach that destination by following the yellow Destination Marker. All of the Mary Jane Missions are fully described in the 'Hero's Work is Never Done' chapter. Mary Jane Missions award large sums of Hero Points, and it should take only one successful mission to net the remaining Hero Points necessary to advance to the next chapter.

CHAPTER WRAP-UP

THERE WEREN'T ANY NEW HERO UPGRADES TO PURCHASE IN THIS CHAPTER, BUT THERE WILL BE PLENTY FOR SPIDER-MAN TO BUY SOON ENOUGH. BUT THAT ISN'T NECESSARILY THE SOLACE HE'S LOOKING FOR AFTER LEARNING THAT MARY JANE WILL MARRY JOHN JAMESON. AND ALTHOUGH BEATING UP ON SHOCKER DID TAKE SPIDER-MAN'S MIND OFF MARY JANE FOR A LITTLE WHILE, SEEING HIM ESCAPE ONLY MADE THINGS WORSE. NOW HE HAS TO DEAL WITH GIRL TROUBLE AND THREE SUPER VILLAINS ON THE LOOSE!

CHAPTER 19:

Cleaning the Slate

To-Do List

- Meet Jameson at the Daily Bugle.
- Earn 4000 More Hero Points.

Mission Objectives

Poor Quentin Beck
Goodbye Shocker

State of the Story

Spider-Man isn't letting the fact that Shocker got away ruin his mood. He knows he can defeat Shocker whenever the opportunity arises and, based on Black Cat's uncanny ability to lead Spider-Man to the bad guys, he's sure to get another chance. After all, he can't worry about some quilt-wearing escaped convict when he has rent to pay and a wedding to stop! It's that whole "two lives" thing again.

POOR QUENTIN BECK

MISSION TYPE

Swing-To

Combat

CHARACTERS INVOLVED

Spider-Man

Peter Parker

Mr. Jameson

Mysterio

Quentin Beck

It's time to pay Mr. Jameson another visit at the Daily Bugle. Perhaps this time he really will have a high-paying assignment for him. Swing through the city to the Daily Bugle office, marked by the white Destination Marker on the screen. It just so happens that Mr. Jameson does have an assignment: Peter needs to get down to the docks to photograph the important dignitary that is rumored to be arriving.

Spider-Man enters the convenience store to find none other than Mysterio harassing the lone clerk behind the counter. After all of the holograms and shenanigans, and all of the empty threats, could it be possibly be that Spider-Man would corner his most elusive prey in a Speedy Mart?

Exit the Daily Bugle via the Change Icon in the restroom, and head due east from the Daily Bugle toward the waterfront. A plea for help from the streets below interrupts Spider-Man's journey. It turns out that alien monsters are invading a nearby convenience store. Only Spider-Man can save the store! Note that the blue Destination Marker now points Spider-Man away from the water and toward the Speedy Mart a couple blocks north.

A lengthy health bar appears in the corner of the screen, and it rapidly fills up several times over, as if to suggest that this alien invader is far too strong for mild-mannered Spider-Man—as if! Spider-Man needs to land only one simple Sprint Uppercut to knock that fishbowl off Mysterio's head and reveal him for who he really is—Quentin Beck!

GOODBYE SHOCKER

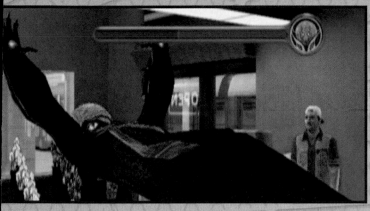

MISSION TYPE
- Swing-To
- Chase
- Combat
- Boss Battle

CHARACTERS INVOLVED
- Spider-Man
- Peter Parker
- Mr. Jameson
- Black Cat
- Shocker Thugs
- Shocker

Spider-Man can't take it anymore. He's decided to rush back into Mr. Jameson's office and demand that he stop printing those lies! A blue Destination Marker appears on the screen to lead Spider-Man back to the Daily Bugle's roof. Scale the side of the building and approach the secret ventilation entrance.

Before Spider-Man can go give Mr. Jameson a piece of his mind, Black Cat arrives on the rooftop and calms him down. She doesn't understand why Spider-Man feels so much responsibility all the time, and she wonders why he doesn't enjoy himself more, but she only has to mention Shocker to get Spider-Man's undivided attention. She heard where his new lair is and she's willing to lead Spider-Man there—if he'll stop groaning about the Daily Bugle!

Spider-Man snaps a few photos of Quentin Beck cowering in the corner near the baby diapers before he exits the store. Another blue Destination Marker appears, guiding Spider-Man back to the Daily Bugle where, hopefully, Mr. Jameson will be willing to pay top dollar for the photos.

THANKLESS JOB

As luck has it, Mr. Jameson assumes that Quentin Beck and Spider-Man are partners in an elaborate hoax and that both of them are enemies of the city. Not only does this annoy Peter who knows the truth, but the people of the city are also starting to hate Spider-Man because of the incorrect reporting in the Daily Bugle. This last fact becomes all too evident when Spider-Man tries to rescue a lady on the sidewalk outside the newspaper building. Rather than thanking Spider-Man for heeding her call, she runs in terror. Word travels fast in this city!

Spider-Man must follow Black Cat once again, but as was the case the last time, she doesn't try to shake him from her tail. Rather, she leads the way at a comfortable pace. The white trail that she leaves in her wake is especially noticeable against the nighttime ambience, so Spider-Man should have no problem following her. Try to stick to the rooftops as best as possible, and be ready with the Sprint Button to Wallsprint or Web Zip whenever necessary.

Black Cat stands back and watches as Spider-Man takes on Shocker's Thugs alone, but she immediately continues the trip to Shocker's newest hideout as soon as the baddies are defeated. Watch for the second group of Shocker's Thugs to attack near the bridge. Then Web Swing across to Roosevelt Island, firing Web Lines at the underside of the Queensboro Bridge. On Roosevelt Island, follow Black Cat north to the abandoned Oscorp research lab.

Black Cat leads Spider-Man to the large bay door on the side of the building. Enter the facility and ascend the stairs to the hallway above. Follow the corridor through the doors toward the yellow Destination Marker. Black Cat found an alternate entrance and is waiting inside for Spider-Man. She's not alone.

The trip across the city with Black Cat isn't as simple and playful as past chases were. Spider-Man has to face a few groups of Shocker's Thugs through the course of the journey. Each is armed with an explosive energy blaster that can inflict moderate damage to Spider-Man, but fortunately they are wearing little in the way of body armor. Use the Web Yank attack to toss them into the air, and then leap up to begin unloading on them with a lengthy air combo. We suggest using the Web Trap against them.

THUG AMBUSHES

Shocker's Thugs attack at two different locations. The first ambush takes place near the helipad atop the tall skyscraper where Black Cat leads Spider-Man. The second ambush takes place in Tudor City, near the Queensboro Bridge.

SHOCKER
Shocker

SHOCKER

BOSS BATTLE: SHOCKER

BOSS ATTACK	DAMAGE TO SPIDER-MAN
Laser Traps	Low
Homing Energy Blast	Low
Energy Levitator	Low
Large Shockwave Attack	High

Shocker has been waiting for Spider-Man to find him inside this abandoned reactor core. This time he has an elaborate energy shield set up to protect him. Additionally, he has several laser traps arranged to keep Spider-Man on his toes, as well as several energy platforms that help lift Shocker off the ground.

Shocker attacks in the same manner as before, but this time Spider-Man has to work with Black Cat to deactivate the force field before he can fight back. Black Cat attempts to deactivate the shield at one of the four control panels in the upper part of the core. Once she figures it out, she calls for Spider-Man to help her. At that time, he must make his way to the control panel on the ledge directly across from Black Cat. Approach the panel and press the Attack Button to power down Shocker's shield.

So long as Shocker is behind his energy force field, he'll rely on the energy blast attack to slowly whittle down Spider-Man's health. At this point, all Spider-Man can do is Web Swing, Web Zip, and Wallsprint around the room to avoid Shocker's attacks and buy Black Cat some extra time. As long as Spider-Man stays on the move and keeps to the upper reaches of the core, he'll avoid most of Shocker's attacks. Press the Grab Button when his head flashes to dodge attacks that might otherwise hit home.

When the shield is deactivated, Shocker is lowered to the floor and is susceptible to the same attacks that Spider-Man used to defeat him in their first encounter. To start dealing the pain, charge the Jump Meter and attack with the Hero Punch or Rising Shoulder Charge (if purchased). Follow him around the arena as close as possible and continue the assault. In an attempt to fight back, Shocker unleashes his massive shockwave energy attack if given the chance. Watch for the lights to flicker, and then scurry as far away from him as possible to avoid the gigantic attack.

Shocker's energy shield doesn't stay down for long, and Spider-Man must resume distracting him while Black Cat again tries to disengage the shield. Listen for Black Cat's signal, quickly get to the control panel opposite her location, and disable the shield. Each time Shocker's shield is disabled, he manages to reactivate it faster and faster, thus reducing the time in which Spider-Man can attack.

As the battle continues, Shocker begins using the same levitating ability that he used to slam Black Cat into the warehouse's ceiling. Fortunately, Spider-Man isn't caught off guard. He can Web Zip away from the energy column's pull. The core becomes slightly more chaotic due to the release of stray energy, but Spider-Man really only needs to worry about avoiding those powerful shockwave attacks. The pods around the floor of the core start to emit the same propulsion energy that Shocker uses to push Spider-Man away from him, but this is more of an inconvenience than a threat.

SPEED ADVANTAGE

Having trouble staying out of Shocker's energy beam? Tired of getting pushed across the core away from Spider-Man's target? Try using the Web Zip to close the distance between Spider-Man and Shocker. If that doesn't work, switch to Spider Reflexes. Everything except Spider-Man slows down during Spider Reflexes. This allows him run straight toward Shocker despite the beam's force pushing him away—Spider-Man will be running faster than the beam can propel him in the opposite direction.

Black Cat says goodbye to Spider-Man and vanishes as soon as the battle is over. Exit the core through the door near the floor, and return outside through the large door that Spider-Man arrived at earlier.

SPIDER-MAN'S FREE TIME

By the time he defeats Shocker, Spider-Man should have most of the 4000 Hero Points he needs to fulfill the To-Do List requirement. Not only did he get large sums of Hero Points for completing this chapter's two missions, but he also earned the "Alien Buster" and "Shock Absorber" awards for ridding the world of two more super villains!

If this is Spider-Man's first trip to Roosevelt Island, there are a number of Buoy and Secret Tokens for him to collect. Also, the island's citizens may offer up some unique Volunteer Missions that Spider-Man hasn't encountered yet. The chapter will end as soon as Spider-Man earns the requisite Hero Points. Speaking of Hero Points, head to an Upgrade Store and purchase the Level 6 Swing Speed upgrade!

CHAPTER WRAP-UP

SPIDER-MAN MAY BE FEELING A BIT MISUNDERSTOOD BY THE PUBLIC, BUT THE FACT THAT HE WAS ABLE TO RID THE PLANET OF TWO SUPER VILLAINS IN ONE EVENING (EVEN IF ONE WAS A FRAUD) IS A GOOD THING INDEED. THROW IN THE FACT THAT BLACK CAT IS REALLY STARTING TO PAY HIM MORE ATTENTION AND THERE'S NO DENYING THAT THIS WAS A GREAT NIGHT TO BE A TIGHT-WEARING SUPERHERO!

CHAPTER 14:

Burning Bridges

To-Do List

- 🕸 Earn 3000 More Hero Points.

Mission Objectives

Meet Mary Jane
Cat Fun
Girl Trouble

State of the Story

Now that Spider-Man has two of his biggest adversaries behind bars, he can concentrate on the troubles in his life, namely the life he leads as Peter Parker. He has a lot of questions and the only person he thinks will understand is Black Cat. After all, what good is having friends who are superheroes if you can't hit them up for relationship advice?

MEET MARY JANE

MISSION TYPE

Swing-To

Combat

CHARACTERS INVOLVED

Spider-Man

Mary Jane

Street Thugs

Spider-Man remembers that Mary Jane is performing in her play again tonight, and he decides that he might be able to make it to the theatre in time to see her. He has 5:00 to get to the theatre in time to see her leave and, depending on where he is when the chapter begins, that should be more than enough time.

Web Swing south through the city toward the blue Destination Marker. The theatre is only a few blocks east of the Daily Bugle and is not hard to reach. Land on the roof of the building behind the theatre where the giant Spider symbol is to wait for Mary Jane.

It's a good thing that Spider-Man decided to swing by to see her, because three street thugs decide to mug her as she leaves the playhouse. Rush to her rescue with Spider-Man, and knock the lowly street scum unconscious with a quick barrage of punches and kicks. None of them are armed, nor are they all that tough, so Spider-Man can whip them into submission within a few short seconds.

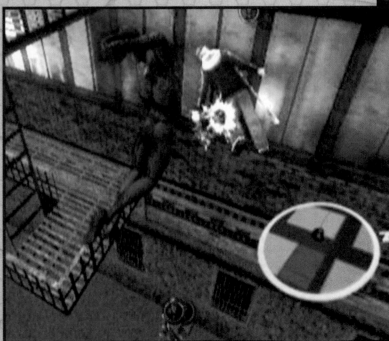

Mary Jane and Spider-Man talk briefly while the thugs lie motionless in the alley. Her explanation for her decision to get married sends Spider-Man's mind wandering and leaves him wondering what could have been.

CAT FUN

MISSION TYPE

Swing-To

Race

Combat

CHARACTERS INVOLVED

Spider-Man

Black Cat

Armored Battle Suits

Criminals

Spider-Man realizes that he needs to talk with Black Cat. She currently sits atop one of New York City's tallest skyscrapers. The blue Destination Marker leads Spider-Man northeast toward the Midtown area. Wallsprint and jump up the skyscraper's side to the ornamental ledges near the top.

After a lengthy discussion about girls, being a superhero, and life in general, Black Cat finally manages to cheer up Spider-Man. She then challenges him to a race across town to the warehouse near the piers in the Garment District.

Black Cat immediately leaps off the skyscraper and speeds off in a northwest direction from Midtown toward the Garment District. A blue Destination Marker points to the finish line and a meter at the top of the screen tracks both characters' progress. Jump off the building after Black Cat, and carefully guide Spider-Man down into the canyon between the nearby buildings before shooting the first Web Line. Web Swing as fast as possible along the wide avenue that leads straight toward the Destination Marker.

Press the Sprint Button near the bottom of the swing for a Swing Boost, and jump from the Web Swing just as Spider-Man begins an upward trajectory. Swing higher before jumping if there is a building to traverse, and then use the Web Zip to catapult Spider-Man forward into his next Web Swing. Black Cat moves pretty fast, but if Spider-Man has the Level 6 Swing Speed upgrade, he shouldn't have much trouble beating her to the finish.

ATTACK OF THE ARMORED BATTLE SUITS

Black Cat leads Spider-Man into position atop the warehouse's roof near the waterfront, and the two eavesdrop on the presentation being given directly below them. Some important criminal types are unveiling three large Armored Battle Suits presumably designed for illegal purposes. Not content to be a silent witness, Black Cat calls out to the crooks and launches the two heroes into the toughest fight Spider-Man has yet to face.

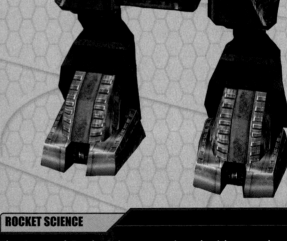

Black Cat immediately leaps down toward the crowd and begins fighting the men with the guns. She doesn't take any damage or die, so it's best to allow her to inflict as much damage as possible in front of the warehouse. In the meantime, head to the right and drop down into the large yard beside the warehouse to take on a smaller number of enemies.

There is one Armored Battle Suit and a sniper on a container in the far corner. Leap through the air toward the sniper, and Web Yank him into the air to unleash an air combo on him. Other gunmen come running around the building's side, but Spider-Man has plenty of time to meet them halfway, near the Armored Battle Suit. Quickly activate the Spider Reflexes and eliminate the gunmen as fast as possible as you try to dodge the incoming gunfire.

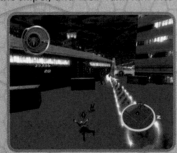

ROCKET SCIENCE

The Armored Battle Suits are equipped with a number of weapons, but it's their rocket launchers that Spider-Man must fear the most. He can avoid them with some fast moving evasive maneuvers, but their blast radius is pretty large so don't expect to simply tap the Grab Button to dodge them.

Focus on the Armored Battle Suit only after the gunmen are defeated, because it takes a number of successful attacks to destroy one of these metallic behemoths. The Armored Battle Suit moves quite slowly, so Spider-Man's best bet is to attack from its blind spot. Try to stay behind it at all times and continue to attack with fervor.

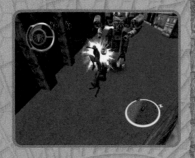

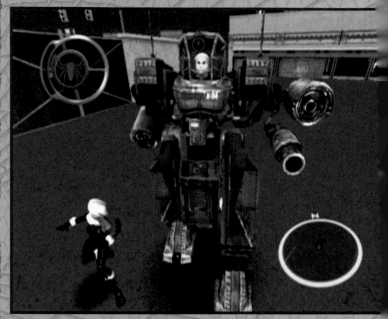

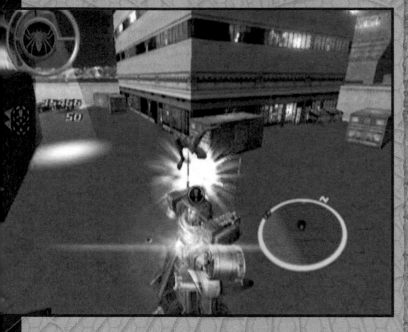

When all the enemies on the side of the warehouse are defeated, leap back to the rooftop, return to where Spider-Man and Black Cat were first positioned, and see how Black Cat is handling the enemies in front. Chances are good that there will still be two Armored Battle Suits to dispatch, but leap down and finish off any remaining gunmen before tackling the larger enemies.

Black Cat helps Spider-Man whittle away at the Armored Battle Suits, but it's up to Spider-Man to inflict the most damage on them. The key is to avoid being caught in a crossfire between the two of them. Attack fast with a Rising Shoulder Charge or Hero Punch, and then Web Zip out of the way to avoid their firepower. The Armored Battle Suits often fire at Black Cat so Spider-Man's head won't necessarily flash before every attack, which makes this final part of the battle difficult. If Spider-Man's close to Black Cat, he could get caught in the blast radius. Continually moving and attacking from their blind spots will virtually guarantee success.

GIRL TROUBLE

MISSION TYPE
Swing-To

CHARACTERS INVOLVED
Spider-Man

Black Cat

Peter Parker

Mary Jane

It doesn't take long after Black Cat leaves Spider-Man at the pier for him to realize that he needs to talk with her some more. A blue Destination Marker appears on the screen to reveal her location. Head northeast away from the waterfront toward her location. Along the way, keep an eye peeled for inactivated Hint Markers or any of the Exploration Tokens that reside in this part of the city.

Spider-Man has a lot on his mind, and once again Black Cat helps him figure some of it out. Thanks to Black Cat, Spider-Man knows he must tell Mary Jane exactly how he feels. A second blue Destination Marker appears on the screen, pointing to Mary Jane's apartment in Soho. Web Swing through the city to her building, and access the Change Icon on the roof to change into Peter Parker's normal attire.

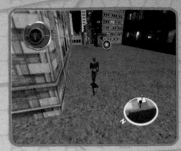

Mary Jane comes to the door and Peter wastes no time telling her how he feels. Unfortunately for him, it doesn't change the fact that she will marry John Jameson. Mary Jane goes back inside and leaves Spider-Man feeling more dejected than ever.

SPIDER-MAN'S FREE TIME

This chapter contained several missions that rewarded Spider-Man with more than enough Hero Points to meet the To-Do List requirement. Nevertheless, there are always crimes to prevent, tokens to find, and Challenges to complete. Use the Zoom Map to locate the nearest Upgrade Store and start heading in that direction.

CHAPTER WRAP-UP

SPIDER-MAN SPENT THE EVENING GALLIVANTING AROUND THE CITY WITH BLACK CAT, BUT HIS MIND WAS ON MARY JANE THE ENTIRE TIME. WELL, EXCEPT FOR WHEN THOSE THREE ARMORED BATTLE SUITS WERE BEARING DOWN ON HIM WITH THEIR ROCKET LAUNCHERS AND LASER CANNONS! WHO WERE THOSE GUYS, ANYWAY? AND WHY DID BLACK CAT FEEL IT NECESSARY TO PICK A FIGHT WITH THEM?

CHAPTER 19:

To Save the City

To-Do List

🔘 Go to Your Apartment.

Mission Objectives

Train Battle
The Final Battle

State of the Story

Revenge can bring out the worst in people. Harry Osborn is convinced that Spider-Man killed his father, and Doctor Octavius blames Spider-Man for the death of his sweet wife, Rosie. Together they share a common, albeit unjustified, craving for vengeance and decide to work together to bring down Spider-Man.

TRAIN BATTLE

MISSION TYPE
Swing-To
Boss Battle

CHARACTERS INVOLVED
Spider-Man
Peter Parker
Mary Jane
Doc Ock

Spider-Man decides that he should head home and check his answering machine. A white Destination Marker guides the way to Peter Parker's apartment. Stop off at an Upgrade Store on the way there to purchase any remaining upgrades that you haven't obtained. Also, make sure that Spider-Man's health is full, otherwise purchase the Full Health upgrade to fill it back up.

The two don't get to talk for too long before Doc Ock arrives to spoil the mood. Not only does he ruin their lunch, but he also kidnaps Mary Jane. He tells Peter to make sure that his friend Spider-Man meets him at the tower in El Barrio if he wants Mary Jane to live to see another day.

It was a good idea to head home, as Mary Jane left a message for Peter to meet her at a nearby café. He has 1:50 to get to the café in time to meet with Mary Jane. Leap out the apartment window and start Web Swinging north to the Flat Iron neighborhood. Follow the main road past the Daily Bugle and toward the enormous skyscraper; the café is on the left. Locate the Change Icon on the roof to switch into Peter's clothing.

Spider-Man returns to the café's roof and finds himself with 1:50 to reach the tower in El Barrio. There's no time to waste—Spider-Man must Web Swing as fast as he can northward past Central Park and the Upper East Side, toward the train tracks in El Barrio. The building that Doc Ock specified is within the lower portion of the train tracks. It's the one with the enormous red sign on top of it.

Doc Ock arrives on the scene without Mary Jane, but he quickly collects a few dozen other hostages—the people on board the train! He leaps onto the speeding train and destroys the control panel at the station, allowing the train to run out of control. Win or lose, he demands that Spider-Man fight him, and Spider-Man has no choice but to comply.

Doc Ock

BOSS BATTLE: DOC OCK

BOSS ATTACK	DAMAGE TO SPIDER-MAN
Tentacle Claw	Low
Tentacle Throw	Low
Tentacle Slam	Moderate
Hit by Train	Very High

The first step in the battle is to get aboard the train safely. Leap down off the rooftop onto the tracks and Web Zip after the train. Sprint along the tracks while charging the Jump Meter, and then launch into a sprinting jump. Have the Jump Meter charged and ready to leap directly into a second jump, and Web Zip onto the train.

THROWN UNDER THE TRAIN

Spider-Man can absorb Doc Ock's attacks fairly well, but even Spider-Man can't withstand being run over by a speeding train. Be extra careful when leaping around on the train, as it is easy fall off in front of it. Should Spider-Man start to fall onto the tracks, rapidly tap the Grab Button to regain control, then Web Zip to a nearby building and hang out there until the train passes. It's safer to catch up to the train than it is to fight Doc Ock with near-fatal injuries.

Spider-Man has already briefly fought Doc Ock once before, so it should be no secret what to expect. He uses two of his tentacles to stay grounded to the train, and he attacks with the other two. You must be extremely observant and dodge the tentacle attacks whenever Spider-Man's head flashes. Sometimes the tentacles will simply slash at Spider-Man, but other times they will pull him high into the air and throw him down onto the tracks.

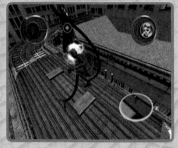 

The key to defeating Doc Ock is to stand a few steps away and wait for him to make the first move. Quickly press the Grab Button to dodge his incoming tentacles. Then immediately press the Web Button to shoot a blast of web juice that temporarily binds his tentacle to the train's roof. Doc Ock quickly attacks with a second tentacle after one is bound, so be ready for it.

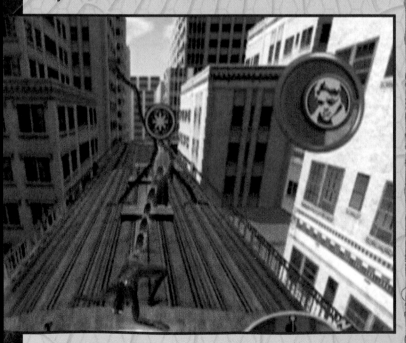

The best way to damage Doc Ock is to sprint toward him and press the Jump Button to fling Spider-Man at him. Quickly begin pressing the Attack and Jump Buttons to unload on Doc Ock with a powerful combo attack. Don't be afraid of getting grabbed by his tentacles. Just remember to repeatedly press the Grab Button to break free of his grasp and to avoid being thrown limply in front of the train.

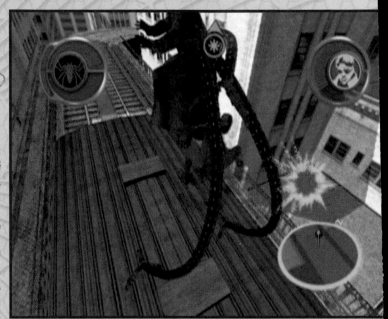

So long as Spider-Man continues to bind up at least one of Doc Ock's tentacles before moving in for the kill, he'll have a good chance of winning the battle. Should Spider-Man consistently bind both of Doc Ock's attacking tentacles, he'll be able to beat on a defenseless Doc Ock and enjoy a very quick victory.

Unfortunately for Spider-Man, victory doesn't come without some pain. Doc Ock gets off the train just as Spider-Man goes to inflict the final blow, and Spider-Man naturally turns his attention to stopping the runaway train. Saving the train's passengers takes all the strength Spider-Man can muster, and he collapses to the ground after doing so. It looks to be Doc Ock's lucky day after all.

THE FINAL BATTLE

MISSION TYPE
Swing-To
Action Puzzle
Boss Battle

CHARACTERS INVOLVED
Spider-Man
Harry Osborn
Doc Ock
Mary Jane

Harry Osborn was about to kill Spider-Man, but his decision to unmask him yielded a shock that caught Harry unprepared. Although Harry doesn't quite know what to think, he was kind enough to tell Spider-Man where Doc Ock may have taken Mary Jane. Spider-Man puts on his mask and goes outside onto the roof; he has 0:55 to get to the abandoned pier in Tribeca. Let the blue Destination Marker be the guide, and Web Swing northwest out of the Financial District and past Civic Center to the abandoned pier. Spider-Man can use an entrance on the dilapidated structure's roof.

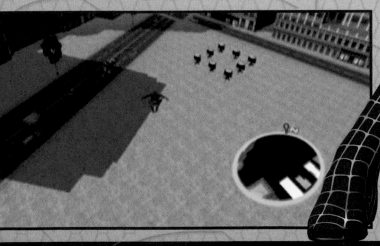

Doc Ock has rebuilt his reactor inside this abandoned wharf and is about to retry his dangerous fusion experiment. Spider-Man sees Mary Jane chained up in the corner and he goes to her, but Doc Ock spots him. Before Spider-Man can do anything, a tentacle slams him into the wall and causes his mask to fall off, exposing his true identity to everyone present.

Spider-Man begins the mission on one of the corner platforms two floors above the water. Doc Ock and Mary Jane are also on this platform. Ignore the nearby control terminal, sprint to the edge, and leap across the room to the neighboring corner platform. Approach the blinking red light and press the Attack Button to deactivate it. There are four corner platforms on this level of the wharf and each one has a control terminal. Loop around the room in a counterclockwise direction, moving from platform to platform to deactivate the first four terminals. Take care to hug the wall as close as possible to stay on the periphery of the expanding energy orb.

Spider-Man must deactivate the reactor by powering down the control terminals, just as he did in Doctor Octavius's apartment. There are nine terminals scattered throughout the wharf that must be turned off. Although each bears a blinking red light and a glowing power cable that leads directly to it, this is not an easy task. Not only is the reactor pulsing as it did in the apartment, but Doc Ock will stop at nothing to kill Spider-Man.

SAVE THE CITY

Spider-Man's primary goal is to stop the reactor from destroying the city. The only way he can do that is to virtually ignore Doc Ock for the time being. Concentrate on avoiding the pulsing energy orb that expands and contracts from the reactor, and look for the occasional head flash to signal an incoming bolt of plasma or a tentacle. The only way to complete this task is to keep moving and to avoid the water under the pier. There are holes in the floor and if Spider-Man hits the water, he'll automatically fail the mission.

Once Spider-Man disables the terminal near Mary Jane (this should be the fourth one that he deactivates), leap onto the brick wall and Wall Crawl toward the ceiling. The fifth control terminal is mounted to the wall high above the reactor. Follow the glowing cables to its location, and step down onto it to get close enough to deactivate it.

The ninth and final control terminal is the hardest to reach safely, as it's mounted to the wall directly above the water. Locate the wooden platform just above the water (below the level with the three rooms), and stand in the corner near the walls to wait for the energy orb to expand. Locate the control terminal in the corner above the water, and run and jump toward it. Quickly Web Zip into a Wall Crawl and deactivate it.

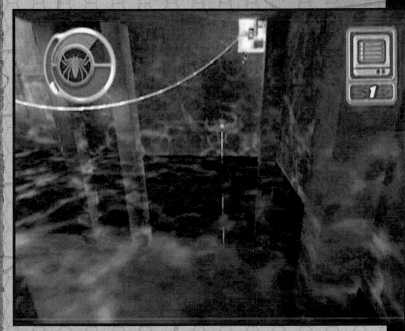

Now, drop down to the lower level of the wharf. There are three side rooms, each of which contains a control terminal. Follow the white and silver glowing cables into each of the three rooms, and deactivate the control terminals found within.

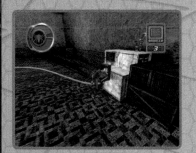

One might think that this would put a stop to Doc Ock's maniacal behavior, but all it does is disable his protective energy shield. Doc Ock is as mad as ever now that Spider-Man has thwarted his plans—he intends to make the superhero pay for it with his life.

Doc Ock

BOSS BATTLE: DOC OCK

BOSS ATTACK	DAMAGE TO SPIDER-MAN
Tentacle Claw	Low
Tentacle Throw	Low
Tentacle Slam	Moderate

DOC OCK, FINAL ROUND

This battle is very similar to the one that took place on top of the train, but with one key difference: Doc Ock is stronger and more aggressive than ever! The good news is that Spider-Man has a lot of room to maneuver, and he's had plenty of experience dealing with Doc Ock up to this point.

From the moment the fight begins, hold your ground on the corner platform, and allow Doc Ock to come to Spider-Man. Activate the lock-on camera to track Doc Ock's whereabouts, and be ready to dodge his tentacle attacks. Follow each dodge with a tap of the Web Button to try to bind his tentacles to the floor or wall.

Try to keep steady pressure on Doc Ock. Don't be afraid to stay close to him, and to try to attack whenever possible. Although Spider-Man suffers some damage from Doc Ock's tentacle attacks, he can absorb a lot of hits before he is in any real danger of being defeated. In fact, Spider-Man's greatest threat may actually be falling in the water. Stay on the corner platform and continue to use the tactics that have gotten Spider-Man this far, and victory will be yours.

SPIDER-MAN'S FREE TIME

Spider-Man has plenty of time to do as he wishes, now that Doc Ock and all the rest of the known super villains are defeated. Enjoy the cinematic, but don't turn off the game just yet. Let the credits play through to advance to Chapter 16. Spider-Man has a new lease on life and it starts now!

CHAPTER WRAP-UP
YOU DIDN'T THINK WE'D SPOIL THE ENDING DID YOU? DEFEAT DOC OCK AND WATCH FOR YOURSELF—YOU WON'T BE DISAPPOINTED!

The First Day of the Rest of Your Life

To-Do List

- Earn 50000 More Hero Points.

Mission Objectives

N/A

State of the Story

If you think, just because you beat Doc Ock and got the girl, that your days of fighting crime are behind you, think again. This is only the beginning. There are hundreds of Exploration Tokens, a multitude of Challenges, and an endless supply of scum-sucking thugs to deal with. And let's not forget that rent still needs to be paid each month!

IT'S ALL FREE TIME FROM NOW ON

That's not a typo; Spider-Man needs to earn 50,000 Hero Points to complete the requirement for this chapter. But don't despair—there are so many opportunities to earn Hero Points, it almost seems unfair.

As if that wasn't enough on Spider-Man's plate, there is an endless supply of citizens in distress to assist. Spider-Man can rush off to stop a Petty Crime in progress, or he can take on a Voluntary Mission from any of the pedestrians with green question marks above their heads. There are almost as many types of Voluntary Missions as there are people in New York City, so don't be afraid to lend a hand. And speaking of lending a hand, the 'Hero's Work is Never Done' chapter in this guide provides all the details and tips necessary to complete all the tasks outlined above.

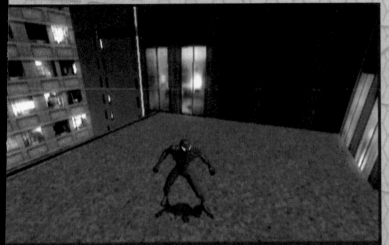

CHAPTER 16

THE FIRST DAY OF THE REST OF YOUR LIFE

First off, there are several dozen Photo Missions, Mary Jane Missions, and Pizza Missions that Spider-Man can complete to earn a lot of Hero Points in a short amount of time. Then there are the Challenges. There are 150 different races scattered throughout the city with each yielding a minimum of 300 Hero Points. Those who want to rack up Hero Points while simply swinging through the city can focus on the Exploration Tokens. The hundreds of Skyscraper, Buoy, Secret, and Hideout Tokens yield thousands upon thousands of Hero Points when collected.

EXT TRICK: ANYTHING

GO SHOPPING!

It's a new chapter, right? That means the Upgrade Store has some new items in stock. Swing by the nearest Upgrade Store to purchase the Level 7 Swing Speed upgrade, the Movie Theatre, and the Fight Arena.

Secrets

Available in Chapter 16

The game isn't over when Doc Ock is defeated; Chapter 16 loads after the credits are finished playing. And with each new chapter comes new items available for purchase at the Upgrade Store.

MOVIE THEATRE

Head to the nearest Upgrade Store and purchase the Movie Theatre for 1000 Hero Points. Now head to the Movie Theatre and activate the Change Icon on the sidewalk to choose from Activision Logo, Treyarch Logo, three demos, and the Credits.

FIGHT ARENA

Another item available at the Upgrade Store is the Fight Arena. Purchase the Fight Arena for 5000 Hero Points, and then head to the Shocker Warehouse near the Lower East Side to partake in these arena battles. Enter the warehouse through the large bay doors. Then cross the first room to the main area where the first battle with Shocker took place. Access the marker to start the rumble.

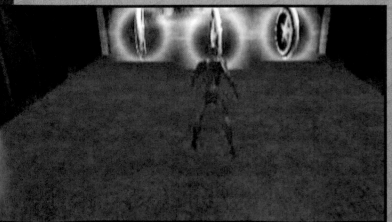

TIMED ROUNDS

When Spider-Man first enters the Fight Arena, there is only one choice of battle available. Timed Rounds require Spider-Man to defeat a certain number of enemies before the timer expires. Since the timer encourages an overly aggressive playing style, each of these missions contains one Health Icon located on the overhead walkway. Switch to Spider Reflexes whenever the meter is full, and never stop ducking and diving!

Timed Rounds

ROUND #	ENEMIES	TIME	UNLOCKS
1	10 Enemies	2:00	Timed Round 2
2	10 Enemies	1:20	Timed Round 3
3	14 Enemies	2:10	Timed Round 4 and Endurance Arena
4	17 Enemies	2:10	Timed Round 5
5	10 Snipers	0:50	N/A

ENDURANCE ROUNDS

Ready for a workout? These battles feature wave after wave of enemies (they appear in groups of eight). Although there is no time limit, there is no Health Icon either. Spider-Man should approach these battles with a bit more care, as the enemies are well armed and will quickly whittle away Spider-Man's health if he's not careful. Don't be afraid to flee to the rafters for a breather or to let your thumbs rest for a moment before rejoining the fray.

ENDURANCE ROUNDS

Endurance Rounds

ROUND #	ENEMIES	UNLOCKS
1	25 Enemies	Endurance Round 2
2	50 Enemies	Endurance Round 3
3	75 Enemies	Endurance Round 4 and Boss Arena
4	100 Enemies	N/A

BOSS ROUNDS

It doesn't get any tougher than this! These eight Boss Rounds pit Spider-Man in a battle against all of the toughest enemies and super villains in the game—simultaneously! There is no time limit. There are no Health Icons, and Black Cat is not here to help you. It's just Spider-Man locked in a room with the meanest hombres he ever sent to the slammer! Take a deep breath, practice that Air Pile Driver, and be ready to spend a lot of time in Spider Reflexes. Good luck!

ENEMIES DEFEATED 0/8

Boss Rounds

ROUND #	ENEMIES	UNLOCKS
1	10 Enemies	Boss Round 2
2	Rhino & Large Chump Thugs	Boss Round 3
3	Shocker & Shocker Thugs	Boss Round 4
4	Calypso & Mirrored Thugs	Boss Round 5
5	Doc Ock & Ock Thugs	Boss Round 6
6	Rhino & Large Chump Thugs with Calypso and Mirrored Thugs	Boss Round 7
7	Shocker & Shocker Thugs with Doc Ock & Ock Thugs	Boss Round 8
8	Rhino, Calypso, Shocker, and Doc Ock	N/A

Available in Chapter 17

ONE FINAL UPGRADE

Still playing? Good for you! Earning those 50,000 Hero Points in Chapter 16 wasn't for nothing. Head to the nearest Upgrade Store and purchase the Level 8 Swing Speed Upgrade. It costs 50,000 Hero Points but is definitely worth it if you want to complete all of the Challenges and other side missions. Spider-Man earns the Speed Freak award as soon as this upgrade is purchased.

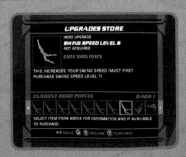

Spider-Man 2™: The Game Mini Walkthrough

INTRODUCTION

Spider-Man 2: The Game for PC goes beyond the film to include extra villains such as Rhino, Puma and Mysterio.

You can control every action in the game with a minimal amount of keys. The standard WSAD setup moves the player in any direction. The spacebar triggers a dodge/block move that is very useful against super thugs and Puma. The right mouse button is used to jump. Double-click to perform a double jump. Note that you can time your second jump to achieve an even greater distance or height. The left mouse button's usage is context-sensitive; it allows you to attack/swing/zip/use/pick up/pull/shoot depending upon the situation. The icon changes to show you what action will be taken depending upon where the cursor is currently aimed. The TAB key brings up the status screen, which displays your health, hero points, spiders collected, and prisoners found. The ESC and Pause keys bring up the pause/menu screen. You can always change your control settings from the *Main Menu > Options > Controls Menu*.

While Wall Crawling, you can hold the spacebar to get a first-person view. From this view, you can Web Zip or Web Swing to areas with ease. While Web Swinging, if you time your release (right mouse button) at the correct point in the swing, you'll be propelled upward at an even greater velocity with an adrenaline boost.

After Mission 1, the player can accumulate and use an adrenaline feature. Every time you dispatch a thug or time your web-swinging correctly, your yellow adrenaline meter (below the health meter) increases. Once it is full, Spider-Man is powered up, and you can now take out any thug with one hit until the meter runs out.

There are six missions in all, with anywhere from one to four maps per mission. Some missions have optional objectives, and Hero Points are rewarded for their completion. Each mission has a certain number of collectible items (exotic spiders and escaped prisoners), which can be found whenever the white Spider-Sense effect appears onscreen. Also, many maps contain glowing blue areas. If the player enters these areas, mini-challenges will begin. These challenges often have Spider-Man collecting, shooting or matching coins, swinging through hoops, or catching would-be purse-snatchers.

TRAINING

This section is straightforward. Just follow Bruce Campbell's instructions, and this should be a breeze.

Mission 1: Rhino Escapes

This mission starts with the gray van chase movie. After the cinema, defeat the two thugs guarding the van, and then walk up to the van. Follow the van, which escapes into the tunnel. Go up and over this building, and continue the chase to the prison.

There will be three waves of thugs to defeat. Rhino then appears. You must jump over his wave attacks, and then move in to attack him up close while he's on the ground. He'll move to the next area, where the police have trapped him. Get him to run at you, and then jump out of the way. When he hits the wall, attack him up close. Continue this until he is defeated.

Mission 2: Ock at the Bank

After the opening cinematic, you must rescue Aunt May. She is located in the closest teller area, in front and to the left of you. Just beat up the four thugs, and she's safe.

Next, you must rescue a security guard. Follow the arrow to the hallway, and then turn to the left. Enter this office, and climb over the pair of short walls to rescue him. Follow the arrow to the security room, and "use" the panel on the side of the door to enter it. There's a control pad below the monitors on the right side; use it to open the upstairs doors.

Once Rhino is gone, the player has some freedom. You can put out the fires by web-pulling the hydrants. There are quite a few blue mini-challenges, and several prisoners/spiders to find. When you are ready to move on, proceed along the street Rhino down which charged, and you'll load into mission 2 (or just follow the large, glowing beacon).

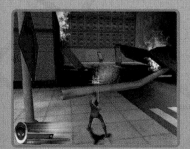

Go back to the main lobby, and go upstairs. There will be one set of doors open. Follow this hallway all the way around to the right, and you'll be in a storage room at the end of the hall. Use the panel on the other side of the room, and climb up into the vents above.

Follow the vent until you reach the green-lit corridor. Then use the panel at the end of this corridor to open the vent. Drop down, and take out the super thug. You can web him up and attack him, or you can wait for the red exclamation mark to dodge his three attacks (by pressing the spacebar). Return to the first floor, and follow the arrow to the elevator. Use the panel, and enter the elevator.

In the basement, follow the arrow to the control room, take out the super thug, and save the guard. Hit the switch on the wall below the monitors to open the door. Follow the arrow to the cash vault, take out the baddies, and rescue the guard in the back-right corner.

Follow the arrow and open the nearby security room. Take out the thug and hit the nearby switch. Enter the nearby precious metals vault, and meet Doc Ock.

Step onto the platform in front of the large door, and web the nodes in the order they are shown to you. After a few of these, the door opens, and you fight Ock. Avoid Ock's attack, and attack him when his tentacles are stuck. You can also pick up the nearby gold bricks and toss them at him. After some time, Ock activates a switch, causing the room to electrify. Get onto something that doesn't conduct electricity, and web-pull the same switch to turn it off. Repeat this process until Ock is toast.

Next, you have to rescue Aunt May from the van. Just get close to the van and web up each of the four tires. Defeat the thugs, and follow the glowing column in the sky to continue to the next mission.

Mission 3: Puma Attacks

Follow Mary Jane's car. It'll stop occasionally to wait for you. Just walk up to it and it'll speed up. Eventually it comes to a warehouse. Walk up to the warehouse to continue. Defeat the thugs, and start working your way up the warehouse. This is a straightforward map; open the doors occasionally and get to the top. At the top, you'll fight Puma.

He's fast, and he sometimes tosses barrels at you. If he picks up a barrel, web his face. When he attacks, beware the exclamation mark combo—dodge three times then counter. Try to counter his every punch, and be ready to dodge his quick counter-counter punches. Eventually, he'll jump out the window. Follow him, and get to the roof.

You'll now chase him rooftop to rooftop. He stops every once in a while to fight. When this happens, use the same techniques as before. Avoid the dropped "W," and follow him into the fountain area. Beat him up some more, and follow him to the construction site.

Enter the building through the same hole in which Puma jumped. Avoid his saw blade attacks, and continue following him or the arrow to catch up to him. You can web up to any of the girders. Whenever you get stuck, use the wall-crawl-look mode to find an area to zip to. When you reach the top, enter the elevator cage match, and fight him the same way as before. His one new attack is to jump off the wall at you. Dodge this attack by pressing the spacebar. Eventually, he'll go down, though an adrenaline-fueled attack will definitely help.

Follow the arrow/glowing column through a few maps, and you'll eventually load into the next mission. You will also be awarded a larger health bar, so you can take twice the punishment!

Mission 4: Assault on OsCorp

Follow the arrow to a large group of thugs, and take them all out. After that, enter the large hole in the wall. Defeat all the thugs in the lobby (including those in nearby rooms), and some gun-toting thugs will appear. After dealing with them, take the open elevator to the second floor.

You must rescue a handful of scientists. Go room to room and do a thorough sweep of the floor. Some doors will unlock only after rescuing a few scientists. The arrow should guide you to most of the cowering nerds. After all the scientists are saved, follow the arrow to the newly opened door, and defeat the super thug. There's one last scientist behind a door. Take out his captor, and he'll open the nearby door to the third floor. Go through this door.

You now have to disarm eight bombs. This is a rather complicated section, so be thorough during your search. Follow the arrow to the first bomb. You will have to jump through some security beams, which will activate the nearby pair of lasers on the ceiling. Hurry through the nearby door. Inside this room is a control panel on the right. Use this to open the cylinder, and then use the item that is now revealed. This is the web-shooter!

Four nearby lasers will activate, but you can now target and shoot them. After destroying the lasers, use the bomb on the other side of the room. You need to web the nodes in the order that they are shown. Once this bomb is disarmed, break through either window into the other room.

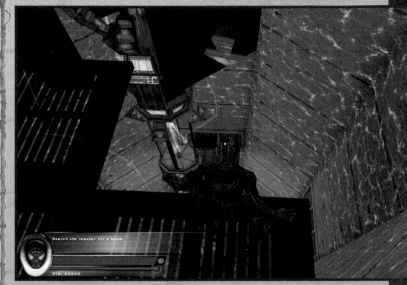

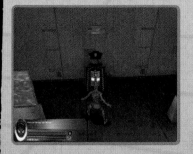

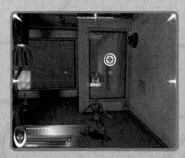

Go all the way down the hallway and hang a left, following the arrow to the next bomb. Open the door into the bomb room, and disarm this bomb. A thug traps Spider-Man in this room and releases a gas attack. So, break through the window on the back wall, and dish out some retribution on this guy.

Return to the hallway, and head to the area with the electrified floor. Zip to the ceiling and Wall Walk your way across this dangerous area. Follow the arrow and destroy the yellow generator box, which opens the next door. Go through this door and enter the first room on the right. Jump to the bottom of the large electrified room, and disarm the bomb there. About halfway up the wall there is a ledge. Zip up to it, and follow the path through some elevators to the next section.

Once back on Level 3, follow the arrow to the bomb that is located in the first room on the right. Disarm this bomb, and then return to the elevator on this level. Destroy the yellow generator box, which opens the nearby red barrier. Follow the arrow through the hall of beams, and enter the first door on the right.

Ock will toss a super thug at you, so deal with him and ascend the stairs. Follow the arrow to the next bomb, which is located in the room at the end of the hallway. Once this is disarmed, follow the arrow to the nearby room with an electrified floor. This floor is controlled by the nearby yellow box generators. Destroy each generator (and the lasers) to clear the room.

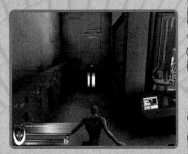

Enter the large room, and prepare for Rhino. Make him charge into all six electrified objects. After that, go into the next room, and Rhino will follow. You must shoot the four liquid nitrogen tanks many times. When they're broken, escape the room fast. Get into the elevator to escape the Maze of OsCorp!

Enter the room inside this room to disarm the next bomb. Follow the arrow through the hallway of double laser beams, and enter the room on the left at the end of the hall. This is a large control room. Take out the thugs and disarm the bomb toward the bottom of the room. Exit the room at the top, and go through the two hallways of laser beams, following the arrow. The final bomb is placed in the first room on the left, in a cove in the corner. Once this is disarmed, follow the arrow back to the room with the previously electrified floor. Take out the new thugs, follow the rescued man to the open elevator, and hop in.

Mission 5: Mysterio's Surprise

Welcome to a new New York. On this level (and the next), you must find a path to the generators that are controlling the mirage. Here are some general tips for finding your way: Use the Web Swing points as much as possible, and time your release correctly to get an added adrenaline boost. Sometimes you have to make leaps of faith—try timing your double-jump so that you get into Web Zip range of your target. If you fall, you'll re-spawn nearby. Finally, don't worry about fighting all the robots; just avoid them whenever possible.

The first map has three generators, designated by large beams in the sky. When you get to the nearby platform, you must take out a robot or three to lower the shield. Shoot the generator (each has two parts), and then move on to the next. When all three are gone, proceed to the exit, which is in the center of the map—follow the arrow.

The second map has only two generators, but they are a bit more sophisticated. When you get to one, a few meteors will fall. Pick up one and toss it onto the platform near the generator's turrets. While the turret shoots at the meteor, jump over and web up the small yellow area on the back of the turret. Once both turrets are disabled, a generator pops up in the middle—destroy it. When both are gone, get to the exit.

The third mission takes places nearly in space. Mysterio brings down a hail of meteors. Wait until they stop falling, and then pick up one and hit Mysterio with it. He may not always bring them down close enough to hit him, so get close to him and wait for the next batch. Do this until he zooms away.

Follow him—there is a series of moving-platform jumps. Pull down the Mysterio statues to form bridges. Continue this until you reach the third large land mass. Follow Mysterio up the Daily Bugle building, and meet his little toy.

Get to a building on the other side of the street, and web-shoot the area where the missiles are originating. When this is destroyed, a green laser appears. Dodge it, shoot the "cockpit." Once that is down, attack Mysterio. Repeat this a few times until he is defeated. Now, onto the final mission!

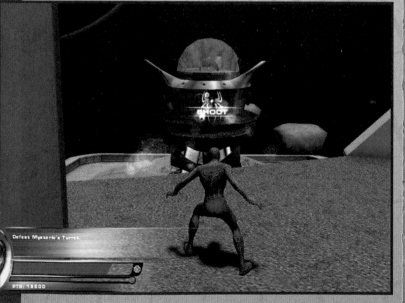

Mission 6: Doc Ock Part II

Ock is escaping on a subway car. You have to wade through the thugs to get to him. The gates will unlock after you defeat roughly two thirds of the thugs. This is a difficult battle. Web up nearby thugs to stop them from attacking, and concentrate on the shooters. You should get your adrenaline up at least once during this battle—make sure you put it to good use. Once the gates have opened, make your way up to the train platforms, and use the swing-rings to get onto the train.

On the train, either avoid or shoot the objects Ock tosses at you. He occasionally disconnects the cars, so be ready to jump when they are getting pulled off. You can Web Zip to the next car if you get propelled too far away. After a few more sequences like this, the train crashes. Your ride is over!

Welcome to the other side of the tracks. If you get into any of the lights, you'll be pelted with laser fire, so avoid them. Avoid the lights and follow the arrow. Open the door with a nearby console and enter the main warehouse. Work your way down, following the arrow, and get into the sewer. Follow the sewer to the end and enter the darkness.

You are now inside Ock's warehouse. Climb up out of the sewers, and avoid the pair of super thugs. There is a hole in the roof here. Jump on up and break the pair of windows. Your goal is to get to the small hole in the wall that the cutscene showed you. You can cling to the brick surfaces, as well as some of the metallic ones. The easiest path is to reach the high area of bricks on the second column, and Crawl Look at the ventilation system. You should be able to zip to it. Crawl over and get into that hole.

Once inside, you'll notice that some walls are discolored. Either shoot or attack them to break through. Follow the obvious path through the warehouse, and you'll eventually see a super thug jump up through a hole in the ceiling. Follow him, and you'll be in the middle of a super thug ambush. This is a tough fight, but try webbing a few of them to buy some time. Eventually, they will run in terror as the reactor starts to come apart. Follow this walkway all the way to the end, and enter the last room. Go up and over the cardboard boxes, and break through the discolored section of the wall. Hello, Mary Jane! Doc Ock's machine blows the room, and the final battle begins.

Web Swing around the platform, and try to get onto one of the raised platforms that surround the center platform. Once there, try to avoid the barrels Ock tosses at you. Web-shoot the crystal that is in the nearest corner. When this is destroyed, a plume of reactor debris rises, knocking Ock silly. Get to the platform and pummel him. Repeat this as often as necessary until Ock is down for good.

Congratulations! You beat Doc Ock, got the girl, and saved the day!

Mini-Games

By reviewing the following table, you'll find out where the mini-challenges are located in the game.

LEVEL	OBJECTIVE
Rhino's Rampage	Collect 50 Red Coins
Rhino's Rampage	Swing Challenge by West Downtown
Rhino's Rampage	Collect: By the Gas Station in Alcove
Rhino's Rampage	Collect: By the Gas Station and Church
Rhino's Rampage	Swing Challenge by Church Tower
Rhino's Rampage	Collect: In Back of Prison
Rhino's Rampage	On top of Brown Building by NW Midtown
8-Armed Robbery	
Inside Bank	Basement Hallway by Vault
Inside Bank	2nd Floor Blue Screen Room
Inside Bank	Basement Room Behind Vault
Inside Bank	Collect: In Soda Machine in First Floor Break Room
Outside Bank	Collect: Across from Swing
Outside Bank	Collect: By the Fountain
Outside Bank	Swing: Across from Collect on Same Street as Bank
Outside Bank	Collect: Corner by Daily Bugle
Outside Bank	Collect: By Southwest Bronx Zone Point
Outside Bank	Collect: By Panda Panda Building
Outside Bank	Swing: On Flag Building. Diagonally across Street from OsCorp
Outside Bank	Swing: On Top of Brown Building across from Daily Bugle

LEVEL	OBJECTIVE
Outside Bank	Purse Snatch: In Alley
Puma Pounces	
City Street	Swing: By Puma Hideout
City Street	Collect: At End of Alley on Other Side of Courtyard
City Street	Swing: On Steps of Weather 99 Building
City Street	Collect: In Alley across from Garage where MJ's Car is Stolen
City Street	Collect: In Cul de Sac by Kung Foos. Diagonal from Museum
City Street	Swing: On Top of Building Behind S.O.S. Billboard
Construction Site	Collect: On Entry Level of Con. Site Building
Construction Site	On Rooftop across Con. Site, Near Bus
Construction Site	Swing: On Rooftop of Building across from Construction Site
Construction Site	Swing: On Con. Site, 1st Outdoor Level
OsCorp Assault	Collect: Lobby
OsCorp Assault	Collect: 2nd Floor by Snacks
OsCorp Assault	Shoot: 3rd Floor Snack Room
OsCorp Assault	Shoot: In Copy Machine Room
Mysterio's Calamity	
Part 1	Shoot: By Oscorp
Part 1	Collect: By First National Bank
Part 1	Collect: By the Fountain
Part 1	Match: Other Side of OsCorp, Left from Spawn Point
Part 2	Shoot: Across from Dinosaur Discovery
Part 2	Shoot By Gas Station, Right from Spawn Point
Part 2	Match: By the Roman Nose
Subway Peril	Match: At Spawn Point
Subway Peril	Match: Center from Spawn Point

Hidden Inmates

The following list reveals where to find escaped inmates.

Rhino's Rampage

INMATE	LOCATION
B. Bad Wolfgang	Under Activision Sign
Sal Berg	Under Gotta Bail Billboard
Werner von Schnitzel	Next to Church, Past Electro-Cage
Barney Rabble	In Alley, Next to Sign of North Downtown
Ditto Coupier	Across Street from Fast Forward

8-Armed Robbery

INMATE	LOCATION
Inside Bank	
Barry Rito	Right of Security Room in Basement
Outside Bank	
Danny Davis	At Bottom of World Investors Building
Jack o Lantern	In Doorway, Down Alley Just Right of Bank
Lloyd Scout	Follow Alley Right of OsCorp
Ira S Banks	Alley Next to Southwest Bronx, in Doorway on the Right
Dave Latick	Building Right of OsCorp, at Top in Doorway of Lower Level

Park Avenue City Street

INMATE	LOCATION
City Street	
Silas Crabtree	On Top of Building w/ Roman Nose
Franklin Beens	On 3rd Level of Bennett Building, on Back Across from Office Space Ad
Slim Sputz	Behind Will Wear Billboard, on Building w/ Cool Garb Ad
Jim Stone	In Far Alley of Courtyard of Last Puma Fight
Brett Stinx	In Puma's Warehouse, First Stairs Down
Construction Site	
Eddie Tuck	In Bottom of Construction Site, Jump over Wall & on Ground Floor
Whaleback Slim	After Building, he's 1st Floor Avenue in Room Where You Have to Attack Frame

OsCorp Assault

INMATE	LOCATION
Warren Peace	In 3rd Floor Elevator

Mysterio's Calamity

INMATE	LOCATION
Part 1	
Manny Hadtoon	On Top of Brown Building, Right of Spawn Point
Part 2	
Bob Simpson	On Top of Old Dyemond Building
Lefty McGrabber	Back of Writz Building

Subway Peril

INMATE	LOCATION
Train Station	
Lenny Boogleschmidtz	In Downstairs Room Left to Spawn Point
Mac Berger	By Train, Up Left Staircase in Room that says Beware of Dog
Docks	
Denny T. Heft	In the 2nd Warehouse. Go Right from Spawn Point.
Vid E.O.R. Cade	In Main Warehouse, 2nd Floor Office B Stairs Down to Tunnel

Final Battle

INMATE	LOCATION
Lester Festerpuss	In Room 1 Up from Spawn Point
Izzy Factur	In Room on Left on Way Out with MJ

Exotic Spiders

In the following lists, you'll discover where to find all of the exotic spiders.

RHINO'S RAMPAGE

- Under the dumpster on the right, just before the prison.
- Under the overhang in the front-left of the prison
- Under the pathway of the hotel building.
- Behind Watrox billboard, which is on top of the building behind the Dyemond building.
- Behind the A/C unit atop the building to the right of the garbage truck that Rhino knocks over.
- On top of A/C unit atop the building next to the building with the Lite Fat billboard (near the electro cage).
- On the left side of the gas station, the side farthest away from the electro cage.
- On top of the round tower at the prison.
- On the back of the hotel building, which is next to the gas station, on the side facing the prison.
- In the alley, on the side of the building that faces the front of the prison.

8-ARMED ROBBERY

Inside Bank

- 1st floor conference room.
- 1st floor office that is only accessible through the vent system.
- 2nd floor in the library, on the ceiling above the hostage in the corner.
- 2nd floor office that is only accessible through the vent system.
- Basement in the 1st mini vault on the left, on top of the safety deposit boxes.
- Basement in the vent system.

8-ARMED ROBBERY (CONTINUED)

Outside Bank

- Behind the fountain.
- Under the overhang at the top of the last building on the right side of the street from the bank.
- On the side of the green building that has the circus advertisement; it's on the right side, roughly three-fourths of the way up.
- On top of the building that is directly behind the One World Investors building.
- Next to the A/C unit on top of the building with the Panda sign.
- In the alley to the right of OsCorp; there is an inmate directly across from the spider.
- In an alcove of the building across the street from the bank. It is on the left side of the building, toward the street sign.
- Under the overhang of the building to the left of the Quick Quourier building.
- On a ledge of the building that is directly across the street from the OsCorp building.
- In an alley, on the ledge of a building near the West Midtown zone point.

PUMA POUNCES

City Street

- On top of the building with the Roman Nose sign and by the Amaze billboard.
- On top of the Benefit building.
- In the middle walkway of the building with the Beuford's Records sign.
- On top of the building with the Two Dogs billboard, which is above the area where the 2nd rooftop battle with Puma occurs.
- On the Pizza Roma building, in the alley on the first ledge from the street.
- On the rooftop of the building behind the Writs building.
- On the building with the Rodeo billboard, on the first walkway level on the opposite side of the billboard.
- Under a dumpster in the alley, across from the garage from which Mary Jane's car exits in the opening cut scene for the level.
- In Puma's hideout, on a girder when you first enter.
- In Puma's hideout, after the room with the 7 thugs. Instead of going upstairs, descend the stairs; there will be a thug and a spider at the end of the path.

Construction Site

- On the street to the right side of the bus, the spider is just past the fountain on the right side of the street.
- Directly to your left after entering the construction site building via the window Puma uses during the cut scene.
- On a girder at the top level, on the opposite side of the entrance to Puma's cage.
- On the crane, on the side facing the construction site.
- On a girder, toward the top of the building. On the corner where the bus is located on the street.
- By the swing mini game that is on the opposite side of the crane. It is behind the satellite dish.

OSCORP ASSAULT

- 1st floor lobby behind the reception desk.
- 2nd floor, from the right of the spawn point, in the room with the purple chamber.
- 2nd floor, in the room with the laser experiment behind the glass.
- 2nd floor, from the right of the spawn point, in the room at the end of the hallway with the servers.
- 3rd floor, before jumping down to deactivate the bomb in the reactor. The spider is on the floor on the opposite side of the opening down to the bomb.
- 4th floor, in the server room, just before the set of four up/down lasers that block your path to the media room.

MYSTERIO'S CALAMITY

Part 1

- On the rock path near the first generator.
- On the rock path near the second generator.
- On the rock path near the third generator.
- On a rock path to the left of the island that has the building with the camel rental billboard. When facing this billboard, the rock path is to the left.

Part 2

- On the bottom of the street island with the meteor craters. This island is one island away from the generator, by the Roman Nose building.
- On the backside of the big rock on the rock path, after you pass the gas station and the next building island.
- In the pipe on the side of the island, to the right of the museum building.
- On the street island between the island with the museum building and the island with the Dyemond building. The spider is next to a pipe sticking out of the island's side.

Part 3

- Under the first island where Mysterio throws rocks at you. Take the rock path down to get the spider.
- Under the island you reach after crossing the first Mysterio bridge. Start the platform jumping section. When you reach the seventh rock, instead of taking the rock to the next Mysterio island, take the other rock and follow the rock path to the spider.
- Under the island after you cross the second Mysterio bridge. Before the next platform jumping section, notice the rock going up and down. Take this rock down and follow the path to the spider.
- During the final platforming section and before you get to the final Mysterio bridge, take the rock down and follow the rock path to the spider.

SUBWAY PERIL

Train Station

- In the kiosk on the main floor.
- On the upper platform, by the door on the left from the spawn point, the spider is on the right side wall.
- On the ceiling of the underground level, to the right of the spawn point.
- On the main floor, between two columns to the left of the spawn point, and under the stairs going to the upper platform.
- On rafter above the main floor, just before you go up the left side stairs toward the train. It is directly under some windows.
- Behind a trash can in the hallway by the stairs you take up to the train.

Docks

- Sitting on crates near the ramp into the main warehouse.
- In the warehouse closest to the spawn point, behind some crates.
- Between forklifts on the ground floor of the main warehouse, near the entrance.
- At the bottom of the roof girder in the main warehouse.
- On 2nd floor of main warehouse next to vending machine, near room with the inmate.
- In the tunnels, under the first set of turrets on your left as you enter the tunnels.

FINAL BATTLE

- In the tower in the electro floor/generator room. You must climb to the top and access the tower from the top of the room. The spider is just after you enter the tower.
- On the top of the vent you use to crawl out of the electro floor/generator room.
- Under the "pull" rock in the sixth room as you go through the rooms while trying to find MJ.
- Under the "pull" mattress, in the room across the hall from the room with the "pull" rock spider.
- On the upper part of the wall, to the left, in the second-to-last room on the floor with all the super thugs.
- On the upper wall, under the roof of the warehouse by the three glass windows.

BRADYGAMES®

X

TENTH ANNIVERSARY

BradyGAMES published its first strategy guide in November of 1993, and every year since then, we've made great efforts to give you the best guides possible. Now celebrating our 10th anniversary, we'd like to take this opportunity to say a few things and extend a special invitation to you—our readers.

First of all, THANK YOU! Whether you're a long-time customer, or this is your first BradyGAMES guide, we appreciate your support. We hope that our guides have enhanced your overall experience when playing games. These days, completing a game isn't just about how quickly you finish. It's about uncovering absolutely everything a game has to offer: side quests, mini-games, secret characters, and multiple endings just to name a few. That's what the *TAKE YOUR GAME FURTHER*® banner at the top of our guides is all about.

Many games deserve more than just a standard strategy guide, and we recognize that. Our guides are produced with the highest quality standards and are tailored specifically for the games they cover. With the introduction of our Signature Series and Limited Edition guides, we raised the bar even higher.

Now for the "invitation" part. Although we constantly challenge ourselves to improve our guides, we'd like your help too. You're formally invited to tell us what you think about our guides. Like something we do? Let us know. Think something we've done is totally lame? Please let us know. We want your feedback no matter if it's good, bad, or just plain ugly. You can write or e-mail us at the addresses below, and we will read what you send. Your opinions are important to us, and may influence the direction for our guides in the future.

Write to:
BradyGAMES
800 E. 96th Street, 3rd Floor
Indianapolis, IN 46240

Send e-mail to:
feedback@bradygames.com

For now, we hope you enjoy this guide. Thanks again for choosing BradyGAMES.

SPIDER-MAN 2™ OFFICIAL STRATEGY GUIDE

By Doug Walsh

©2004 Pearson Education

BradyGAMES® is a registered trademark of Pearson Education, Inc.

BradyGAMES® Publishing

An Imprint of Pearson Education
800 East 96th Street, Third Floor
Indianapolis, Indiana 46240

ISBN: 0-7440-0393-8

Library of Congress Catalog No.: 2004106941

Printing Code: The rightmost double-digit number is the year of the book's printing; the rightmost single-digit number is the number of the book's printing. For example, 04-1 shows that the first printing of the book occurred in 2004.

07 06 05 04   4 3 2 1

Manufactured in the United States of America.

ABOUT THE AUTHOR

Doug Walsh lives in Bellevue, Washington with his wife and two dogs. This is the twenty-ninth strategy guide that he has written for BradyGames. Some of the other recent Activision titles that Doug has worked on include *Tony Hawk's Underground*, *Tenchu: Return from Darkness*, and the PC release of *True Crime: Streets of LA*.

AUTHOR ACKNOWLEDGMENTS

This book would not have been possible without the help of Justin Berenbaum and Irwin Chen of Activision. We greatly appreciate your willingness to support this project during very busy times. Tremendous thanks go to my editor, Tim Fitzpatrick, and to Dan Caparo, Mike Degler, and Leigh Davis of BradyGames for working so hard to put out the best book possible. It's always great to work with you all. I'd also like to thank my lovely wife Kristin for keeping me well caffeinated during my late nights with Spider-Man and for offering to lend a hand whenever possible, even if its usually impossible. Lastly, I'd like to thank our friends Ryan and Kari for not minding when my work schedule goes from abnormal to chaotic.

ACTIVISION STRATEGY GUIDE CREDITS

ACTIVISION

DIRECTOR, BUSINESS AND LEGAL AFFAIRS
Greg Deutsch

BRAND MANAGER
Mike Chiang

ASSOCIATE BRAND MANAGER
Roy Alojado

MANAGER, BUSINESS DEVELOPMENT AND LICENSING
Justin Berenbaum

SPECIAL THANKS TO:
Dani Kim
Allison Gershon
Dave Anderson

PRODUCTION

John Sweeney
Alex Garcia
Chris Archer
Juan Valdes
Matt Powers
Irwin Chen

ACTIVISION Q/A

Ian Moreno
John Rosser
Joe Favazza
Hugh Bach
Josh Chandler
Lee Cheramie
Teak Holley
Aaron Justman
George Ngo
Jacob Porter
Randy Guillote

PC PRODUCTION TEAM

Robert Berger
Kelly Byrd
Bryan Jury
Matt Morton
Chris Archer

TREYARCH

CREATIVE DIRECTOR
Tomo Moriwaki

TECHNICAL DIRECTOR/DESIGNER
Jamie Fristrom

ART DIRECTORS
Alexandre Bortoluzzi
James Chao

TECHNICAL DIRECTOR
Michael Vance

LEAD GAME DESIGNER
Aki Akaike

CHIEF ENGINEER
Jason Bare

CHIEF ANIMATOR
James Zachary

CHIEF TEXTURE ARTIST
Chris Erdman

ARTISTS
Arnold Agraviador
Cameron Petty
Chief Modelers
Barbara Krug
Erik Drageset
Michael Mcmahan

ANIMATOR
Ryan Duffin

AUDIO DIRECTOR
Tom Hays

PRODUCERS
Jeremiah Maza
Jonathan Zamkoff

SENIOR PRODUCER
Gregory John

EXECUTIVE PRODUCER
Bill Dugan

BRADYGAMES STAFF

PUBLISHER
David Waybright

EDITOR-IN-CHIEF
H. Leigh Davis

MARKETING MANAGER
Janet Eshenour

CREATIVE DIRECTOR
Robin Lasek

LICENSING MANAGER
Mike Degler

ASSISTANT MARKETING MANAGER
Susie Nieman

TEAM COORDINATOR
Stacey Beheler

CREDITS

TITLE MANAGER
Tim Fitzpatrick

SCREENSHOT EDITOR
Michael Owen

BOOK DESIGNERS
Dan Caparo
Doug Wilkins

PRODUCTION DESIGNER
Tracy Wehmeyer

ACKNOWLEDGMENTS

BradyGAMES would like to thank everyone at Activision, Treyarch, our friends at Sony Pictures Consumer Products, and MARVEL for an incredible Spider-Man game. Very special thanks to Justin Berenbaum, Irwin Chen, Robert Berger, and Bryan Jury for their expertise and gracious assistance during the making of this guide. Thank you very much!

SPIDER-MAN 2™
THE GAME
OFFICIAL STRATEGY GUIDE